Hazel Hall

The
Upbeat
Generation

CLAIRE COX

HOW AMERICA'S YOUTH IS MEETING THE CHALLENGE OF OUR AGE

PRENTICE–HALL, INC., Englewood Cliffs, N. J.

THE
UPBEAT
GENERATION

By the Same Author

THE NEW-TIME RELIGION

to Nana, with love

Acknowledgments

IF EVERY PERSON AND ORGANIZATION THAT CONTRIBUTED TO this book were to be recognized here, we would have another entire volume. My thanks, therefore, to all those mentioned in the text, who were unstinting in their provision of the necessary data.

There are a few persons to whom I would like to give special mention because of their unusual enthusiasm for this project.

Jack Burkhart of the National YMCA and Louisa Wilson Hager of the National YWCA made themselves available for replies to all sorts of queries. William Parish of the Young Presidents Organization and James Barrett of Junior Achievement were most helpful.

Representatives of the Boy and Girl Scouts, Rebel Robertson and Frances Dale, respectively, came up with much rich material, as did Mary Reinhart of the Boys' Clubs of America, Otho De Vilbiss of the Elks, Fern S. Kelley of the 4-H Clubs and Lois Oliver of the Future Homemakers of America. Alvin L. Schorr of the Social Security Administration not only dug up interesting material but directed me to other sources. The Very Reverend Monsignor George A. Kelly, director of the Family Life Bureau of the Roman Catholic Archdiocese of New York, got a late start on a vacation in order to grant me an interview.

To Elma Williams, Sam M. Lambert and Wilda F. Faust of the National Education Association my special gratitude for long-suffering patience in answering my many and often uneducated queries.

A special word should go also to George Perry of the National

Jewish Welfare Board, Jo H. Chamberlin of the Nutrition Foundation, Ruth M. Leverton of the Institute of Home Economics, Louis C. Jurinich of Optimist International, Robert Walters of the U. S. National Student Association, Marion Simon, formerly of the Association, and Roy C. Cahoon of the Treasury Department.

During the course of preparing this book I had occasion to call upon several old friends for data. Robert Wallace, special assistant to the Secretary of the Treasury, was a friend indeed when I needed help in obtaining some hard-to-get information from another department. Max Rosey provided considerable background for the chapter on young beauties. Charles S. Zurhorst of the Institute for Nutrition Education produced ideas that prompted the writing of the chapter on teen-age nutrition.

To my agent, John Tiffany Elliott, once again, many thanks.

The biggest "thank you" goes to my severest critic and dearest copy reader, my husband, Max L. Lowenthal, Jr.

C. C.

Table of Contents

The
Upbeat
Generation

.1.

The Upbeatniks—A Profile

THERE ARE NO HORIZONS IN THE SPACE AGE. NEW FRONTIERS abound on the bottom of the ocean, on the face of the moon and in atomic laboratories, automated factories and push-button homes. The horizons are gone and there is no ceiling on adventure or achievement. Not even the sky is the limit any more.

Today's teen-ager will pilot a nuclear-powered aircraft around the world or be a pioneer voyager to the moon. He will find new cures for old diseases, build highways that automatically steer cars or invent some marvelous new device for a use no one has ever dreamed of.

It is said that any boy can grow up to be President of the United States. So, too, can anyone become a millionaire. The youngster of today is more likely to have the opportunity to build a fortune than his father did, despite the complaints of many elders that it no longer is possible to become a self-made success. The tycoon who already is well on his way to his second million and not yet 30 will run for public office and then become tomorrow's "elder statesman" when he is scarcely past middle age.

This is the picture of youth today—the uphearted generation—a generation of young people serving the nation and the world, from missionary outposts in Africa to the White House. The accent on youth is a result of the population explosion, prosperity and better schooling for more persons. It may also be an admission of failure on the part of the generations that

1

bumbled into two World Wars and a major depression. In any case, the largest population groups are the very old and the very young. The senior citizens seem to have no objection to giving youth a chance to try to straighten out the world, and the middle segment of American society may have no choice in the matter.

When John F. Kennedy, at 43, became the youngest man elected to the Presidency and proceeded to appoint a number of still younger men to serve with him, there was much talk of a "new day for youth." Actually, Kennedy's election may have been more a result than a cause, for he was riding the crest of a wave of youthful exuberance. As one of the men who had won World War II, he wanted to try to win the peace. Had his opponent, Richard M. Nixon, been elected, he, too, would have ranked as one of the younger presidents.

However, Kennedy and his "New Frontier," with its Peace Corps, revived Civilian Conservation Corps and various other appeals to the young, have enhanced the status of youth. The presence of a young man in the White House has made it more likely that young people across the country will be listened to —respectfully—by their elders.

There are 85,000,000 Americans under 30. Subtract the juvenile delinquents and the beatniks and you have the upbeat generation, well over 80,000,000 strong. Considerable unwarranted notice has been taken of the beat generation, which actually never has existed except in the minds of Jack Kerouac, the noted non-writer, and a handful of indolent admirers of his insolent prose and the literary garbage dumped on the public by the self-styled poets who gather around him. The unkempt low priests of nihilism are the inheritors of the earthy ways of the Bohemians of the 1920's, who also stopped taking baths, advertised themselves as practitioners of "free love," and dedicated their lives to rugged non-individualism. They were the "lost generation," which, like the beat generation, really existed as a social class only in novels.

Beatniks who combine fornication and sloth in Greenwich

Village look upon themselves as individualists, but they are more sheeplike than many a "neatnik" living in split-level tidiness in suburbia. You need the names and numbers of all the players to tell one beatnik from another. The "beat" men hide under a camouflage of beards, turtle-neck sweaters and skin-snug slacks. Their women disfigure themselves with long, stringy hair and "uniforms" that would have made the old-fashioned girl's middy-and-skirt school garb look like a Christian Dior creation.

The distaff beatnik, in her black stockings, shapeless skirt and sweater and bangle earrings plucked from a chandelier, lolls with her beat boy friend in near-squalor while they ridicule the rest of the world and reassure each other that *they* are the only hope left for individualism.

Beatniks scrounging for marijuana and decrying the state of the world in their ghettos on San Francisco's North Beach and in New York's Greenwich Village have given a shabby reputation to other young people by being over-advertised to the world. Meanwhile, the uncelebrated upbeatniks—"squares," according to the beats—are hard at work, wherever there is work to be done. The upbeats, who may be the real individualists of our times, have become involved in a widening circle of constructive, humanitarian activities that reach into homes and communities across America—and around the world.

Perhaps some of the good works of this new uphearted generation seem insignificant and even trivial. But when considered in their entirety, they provide a picture of industriousness and altruism that is indeed impressive.

Many youngsters collect money for fund drives and they get out the vote even though they are not old enough to cast ballots themselves. The simple act of turning the usual Hallowe'en "trick-or-treat" night into an occasion to raise money for underprivileged children overseas has won widespread adult support for United Nations activities that some viewers-with-alarm had branded as Communistic. Teen-agers give their summers to hard labor in work camps at home and abroad, often paying their own expenses to dig ditches, paint churches, repair facilities at mental hospitals or serve as nurses' aides. They read to blind persons and take the aged on outings. Saturdays, evenings and summers are devoted to study in science laboratories without grades or credits.

Quite a few of the more enterprising youngsters have gone on to success in science or business. New fortunes have been made in real estate, foreign cars and electronic devices for moon rockets by the more adventurous ones. Career satisfaction, instead of large sums of money, is an achievement preferred by others, as in the case of the growing number of teachers— particularly those who accept posts in underdeveloped nations. Once on their way to whatever their kind of success may be, the young people—teachers or tycoons—often give part of their leisure to good works, especially to helping those younger than themselves get ahead.

College boys still engage in occasional "panty raids" on girls' dormitories or have contests to see how many football players can be crammed into a telephone booth. But there is no re- corded case of goldfishes being swallowed on a campus since the fathers of today's college boys turned in their beanies, and many fraternity "hell week" hazings have evolved from medieval tortures to public-spirited campus clean-up campaigns or Community Fund drives.

There are those who persist in deploring what they call America's child-centered culture, in which suburban mothers serve as chauffeurs for their offspring and nearly all activities in the home are built around what children do, say, want and eat. The critics are afraid that the world soon will be overrun, and possibly *run,* by young people. If numbers alone are cause for alarm, such worries are well-founded, for the 1960 U. S. Census disclosed that gains among the younger segment more than offset any increase in the older population. This has resulted in the first drop in the median age in the nation's history. The figure in 1960 was 29.5, as compared with 30.2 in

1950. There is every chance of another drop in the 1970 census.

The total under 18 was 64,200,000, as compared with 46,-900,000 for the previous census, in 1950. The "official" teen-age population is expected to rise to 32,000,000 by 1966.

Just what constitutes a teen-ager depends on who is doing the categorizing. As far as legal classification is concerned, there is no such person as a child any more; there are only infants, pre-teens, teens and young adults. Apparently the pre-teen is anyone formerly known as a child who is able to stand but is under 12 years of age. Some persons insist, however, that for social reasons anyone over ten is a teen-ager. Young people start bristling at being called teen-agers when they reach the age of 15. From then on, they prefer to be known as "young adults."

It is apparent that whatever they are called or call them-selves, youngsters, because of their numerical force, are the most sought-after group in the population. The estimated 25,000,000 teen-agers have about $10,000,000,000—that's billions —to spend every year, and competition for this bonanza is keen among the manufacturers of phonograph records, chewing gum, cosmetics, bowling balls, soft drinks and any other product in which young people might be interested. The teen-age market is growing constantly and the teen-ager is more inde-pendent than ever. He earns much of his own money and he decides what to do with it, an affluence and independence that have resulted in expanded motivation research to determine what teen-agers will buy and why.

The largest concern in the field is the Eugene Gilbert Youth Survey, started in 1945 when Gilbert himself was an upbeatnik with hopes of creating a better understanding of the expanding youth market. Gilbert wanted to go into business for himself and to develop a new "product." His willingness to take a chance paid off with considerable financial reward and renown for himself, as well as many insights into the teen-ager as a consumer.

Gilbert believes the teen-age segment of the population may have the largest purchasing power and the greatest influence on marketing. Not only does a youngster decide what he wants for himself, but he also influences family decisions on where to live, what kind of car to buy and what foods to obtain at the supermarket.

The wooing of teen-agers—for their support and for their dollars—is ardent. On the political front, Senator Barry Goldwater devotes much of his time to appealing to the growing conservative element in college student bodies—the voters of tomorrow, and, more precisely, of 1964. Even more conservative —reactionary is a better word—is the John Birch Society, which carries its program to teen-agers and college students as well as older persons. To counter such movements, the Young Republican and Young Democratic organizations are moving ahead with more encouragement from old-line party leaders than ever before. Possibly the most flattering approach to youth has come from a group of senators who want the legal voting age reduced from 21 to 18 to bring more upbeats into the electorate.

Appeals to the intellect are made through teen-age book clubs and successful magazines published mainly for young persons, among them *Mademoiselle* and *Seventeen*. Clifton Fadiman, in analyzing young people's reading tastes for *This Week,* said that teen-agers had about the same preferences as adults; they read the best-sellers, although sometimes ten or fifteen years later.

Radio and television programs by and for youth are growing in popularity to such an extent that several major networks have introduced news programs they hope will attract young audiences. These shows do not "talk down" to youth; they present subjects in which youngsters are presumed to be interested. Robert Abernethy, a commentator assigned to one of the programs, spent part of a summer taking a high school course so he could find out more about young people and their interests. What he learned for his National Broadcasting

Company program, "Update," was that there is scarcely any real difference between the interests and level of understanding of teen-agers and adults. Those from homes with bright and alert parents were themselves bright and alert. Dull parents tended to produce dull classmates for Abernethy.

Young audiences are considered also by producers of entertainment fare on television. Any regular drama must have at least one young hero or it is "dead" for the family viewing audience, as the aging actor Robert Taylor found out when he was obliged to accept a young co-star on his show or face the loss of his teen-age audience. Taylor and others of his vintage are safe in homes with two TV sets, but where there is only one the younger viewers too frequently get their own way.

Juveniles are the darlings of the manufacturers of any product that is wearable, eatable, giveable or designed for family use. When a soft-drink company considered putting its product in cans, it made a survey that caused it to drop the idea; youngsters said they preferred to sip their pop from bottles. A soup company bypassed parental preferences to study the food likes and dislikes of children from 6 to 14 in deciding what to try to sell their mothers in supermarkets. Special cosmetics for youngsters have been so successful that a fifth of the industry's output is bought for or by them, although almost nothing about the products is different from those their parents use except packaging and possibly, name. An "in-depth" study was made in an effort to create a market for hope chests among teen-age girls, and a hosiery company conducted a special campaign to reach girls about to slip into their first nylons. Teen-agers were put to work by an enterprising shoe company helping to design new styles in footwear—for teen-agers.

As a boon to parents and children alike—and to itself—the American Telephone and Telegraph Company took cognizance of the gabbiness of teen-agers by establishing special rates in several states for youngsters who wanted their own telephones and also wanted to pay for them.

No effort has been spared to pierce the "blue denim curtain." So many surveys and analyses have been made of youth, in fact, that *The Catholic Digest* felt compelled to run a survey of youth surveys. The compilation reported, among other things, that high school students had indicated that the elements most important to them in choosing careers were: "Is the job interesting and is the job enjoyable?" Other considerations, in order of importance, were job security, good working conditions, salary, advancement, prestige, fringe benefits and independence.

University and college employment placement officials generally agree that college graduates rank job elements in about the same order teen-agers do. Salary seldom is at the top of the list. Status is an important job requisite; young people feel there is much to be said for working for a company with a big name, even in a little job.

Numerous investigations have been made in the teen-age field. In commenting on the importance of the junior members of society, University of Michigan researchers informed the Boy Scouts of America that Americans live in a youth-centered society influenced in every aspect by teen-agers. The tastes of young people influence the tastes of their elders, whether in language, clothing, music or sports. The adult world is so preoccupied with the new generation, the researchers concluded, that even literature is filled with phrases such as "make way for youth" or "youth will be served."

The report found that the solicitude for the needs of youth had a paradoxical aspect. Childhood dependence is extended in America far beyond the age at which young people in other countries are required to earn their own livelihoods. Parents go to considerable lengths to spare young people from adult responsibilities and even tend to exclude them from realistic roles in the world of grown-ups. Much leisure is afforded teen-agers, the Michigan sociologists said, and yet the adults who provide this luxury worry overtime about what is done with it.

Almost identical studies were made for the Boy and Girl

Scouts by the University of Michigan Institute for Social Research. Comparing the results of the two, the researchers found that boys tended to worry more about achievement than anything else and were more likely than girls to have this preoccupation. The chief worry of girls was "personal characteristics." Second on their list was "acceptance by others." Only 21 per cent of the girls thought much about achievement. Boys said they felt most important and useful when assuming adult roles at home. Girls were slightly less interested in this area but were more inclined to be helpful and more demanding of recognition from adults for their helpfulness.

A number of boys and girls found someone in their families to admire. In most cases, girls wanted to be like their mothers and boys like their fathers. They admired "personal qualities related to the individual." Boys were influenced by the skills of their heroes, while the girls cited what the researchers called "superficial characteristics."

The report on Girl Scouts noted that women live in an inconsistent world. As girls, they are encouraged to pursue personal goals much the same as those set for boys; as women they are expected to have mainly feminine aims. They are taught—and expected—to compete with other girls in achievement and in development of skills. Increasingly, they are expected to become economically independent or to be able to earn their own livelihoods if necessary. But at the same time that they are being prepared to compete in a masculine world, they are expected to develop womanly ways. They are told it is not feminine to become aggressively competitive and are warned they must not become too involved in their own ventures lest their husbands disapprove.

Girls, the report further indicated, run their own lives in many respects, including working after school in jobs of their own choosing, managing their own money and selecting their own clothes. This independence carries over to college and post-college days. A generation or two ago, a girl was likely to go home to her parents after graduation from college and remain there until she married, even if she took a job. Now it is more or less expected that a girl who does not marry immediately after finishing college will leave home and go to work for a time. Many of these young women plan to return to work after their children are well along in school. They regard their employment, whether professional or clerical, as "jobs," not "careers."

This was the gist of the Girl Scout study of the teen-age girl. An analysis of the organization teen-age boy, provided in the earlier phases of a six-year study of members of the Boys' Clubs of America, found that more than half the boys from 14 to 18 had something to worry about—mainly school work— but also personal pressures such as family problems, money, or the future. Achievement in jobs or vocations bothered a small number. Only 5 per cent said they had absolutely no worries, but nearly half acknowledged that they would like to change something about themselves—to become more able, better-tempered, handsomer or friendlier. Fathers were the persons nearly half of these boys admired enough to emulate, but 28 per cent said they just wanted to be themselves.

One significant finding was that boys ranked industriousness over either independence or conformity. Hard work was their goal. This seemed to confirm the results of another study, which concluded that youngsters who were busiest with activities outside the home and school also were doing the greatest amount at home. Furthermore, students who engaged in extracurricular activities tended to come from the happiest and most congenial homes.

The surveys, studies and analyses go on and on. Students themselves scrutinized the 400,000-member college class of 1961 and syndicated what they learned in alumni magazines. Among the bits of miscellany turned up was that 1961 graduates were interested in service overseas, but not necessarily in the Peace Corps. Some preferred the idea of serving as individuals, teaching in foreign schools or being sent abroad by American companies rather than representing the United States Government in basically propagandistic jobs. This finding could be amended to state that college students today generally are more interested in the teaching field than ever before, whether in Des Moines or New Delhi. But pre-medical study is in a slump, as are the pursuits of the fine arts and economics. Foreign languages are on the upswing, but the study of English grammar and spelling has declined to such an extent that even Vassar does not require its students to take courses in English.

Ever the center of attention, young people are not necessarily an object of praise. They have gone through some difficult periods since the end of World War II. First came the Cold War and a sharpened youthful awareness of the world and its problems, which stimulated a desire to be of service. Then came the late Senator Joseph R. McCarthy and his indiscriminate campaign against Communism. Young people were discouraged from action. A cloud hung over politics and public service. "Let someone else do it" was the prevailing attitude.

The intimidation of youth was one of the less publicized but more serious mischiefs committed by McCarthy. Before his rise, youngsters had taken on some of the old-fashioned pioneer spirit; they wanted to change the world. McCarthy frightened them into sullen silence. They became cautious, afraid to speak their minds. All they wanted was to be left alone.

Since his decline and death and the end of the era of hysteria he instigated, young people have been emerging from their psychological fall-out shelters. Their venturesome idealism is returning, as demonstrated in the response to the call of the Peace Corps and the well-established programs of overseas aid on which the corps was based. During McCarthy's heyday, youngsters came to resent anything critical of the United States; they did not know quite how to reply, and they were afraid to. Those who go forth now to serve industry, school, church or nation no longer have such qualms. They have confidence that what they are doing is right. They have ready replies for critics of their country instead of frightened silence or cries of resentment. They are the Upbeat Generation.

.2.

The Case for Teen-Agers

"Don't be a J. D.!" the posters plead.

President Kennedy calls for a $10,000,000-a-year "total attack" on "J.D."

J. Edgar Hoover warns that "J.D." is increasing far out of proportion to the rate of population growth.

This "J.D." is Juvenile Delinquency, but there is another kind of "J.D." that the headline hunters seldom mention.

It is Juvenile Decency.

Only 2 to 5 per cent of the 25,000,000 teen-agers in the United States are delinquents, and they come from a still smaller percentage of the total number of American families. In one large city, for example, a mere one per cent of the families were responsible for 75 per cent of the juvenile delinquency reported in a single year.

The remaining 95 per cent of the young people are what is being called "Juvenile Decents." Premier Khrushchev has called them "dissipated" and "good-for-nothings." Former President Truman says that "they are our best hope for the future."

These young people are engaged in projects to improve their homes, schools, communities, the nation and the world. They help old people fight loneliness. They draw up social and moral codes for teen-agers and adults alike. They work in hospitals, libraries and museums as volunteer aides. They even help each other.

It is no wonder, then, that the upbeat youngsters are stung

12

by every headline they read about delinquency. They agree that juvenile crime is a scourge that must be combated, but they wish it could be dealt with in such a way as to dispel a growing tendency to cast suspicion on all teen-agers, innocent as well as guilty.

President Kennedy, a success symbol of the younger generation, set off bitter complaints by teen-agers when he asked Congress for a five-year program of government leadership in "prevention and control of youth offenses," to cost $10,000,000 in the first year alone.

"How much is President Kennedy going to spend on us?" asked an angry young woman exercising in a YWCA gym.

"Why can't someone say a good word for us?" inquired a high school boy who was building a record player for a blind woman.

There are other questions. "Why don't people think about the fact that most of us are nondelinquents who want to lead natural, normal lives?" "Why doesn't anyone give us credit for being a thinking generation, trying to do something constructive?"

Why not, indeed, agreed Richard A. Orozco, 16, a student at Theodore Roosevelt High School in Los Angeles. In reply to the question, "What are the biggest problems facing teen-agers today?" he wrote a letter to *American Youth* magazine (published by General Motors for 1,500,000 teen-agers) saying that the most irritating problem was that of the bad reputations inflicted on all teen-agers by a small number. Richard said all teen-agers were blamed when some were caught breaking the law. He and his friends ran into constant questioning when they tried to convince adults that they were "all right."

His comment was directly in line with the response of more than 1,000 teen-age delegates to the 1961 annual meeting of Junior Achievement. They agreed overwhelmingly that there was an excessive emphasis on juvenile delinquency. Scholastic magazines received a strong response from teen-agers who complained that movies inaccurately portrayed teen-agers as hood-

lums in leather jackets. Some of the protesters pointed out
that the average law-abiding teen-ager is an unknown quantity
to most adults because he does not make good movie, television
or newspapers fare. In his goodness he is "dull." Little publicity
is given to the good works of teen-agers and too few adults take
cognizance of the fact that the very persons they criticize will
be running the world of tomorrow.

One reason, of course, why teen-agers are discussed so
extensively is that there are so many of them. Adults complain
that youngsters watch too much television and drive too fast—
but then everyone does. Children are criticized for spending
too much money. The persons who put them on the defensive
are grown-ups who themselves are big spenders. "Juvenile delinquent" is a term so loosely used that it covers even the most
playful Hallowe'en prankster. But still worse is a label that has
worked its way out of sociological gobbledygook and into every
day language—"pre-delinquent." Sociologists rush into neigh-
borhoods overrun with children and frantically go to work on
the "pre-delinquents." These are children that the "experts"
have decided are *destined* to become delinquents.

"Pre-delinquent" has become part of the language at a
time when many persons are trying to encourage more discriminating use of "delinquent." Even J. Edgar Hoover, the nation's
chief hand-wringer over the transgressions of youth, agrees that
the label "juvenile delinquent" should be abolished. He sug-
gests such terms as "juvenile crime" or "youthful criminality."
Despite his periodic statistical alarms on the seriousness of the
youth crime situation, Hoover makes it clear that he regards the
bulk of American youth as fine, upstanding citizens.

"I have always cautioned against unjustified criticism of the
overwhelming majority of our young citizens," he says.

He acknowledges also that youngsters too often are put on
the defensive by the wrongdoings of others.

Several positive approaches are being taken to improve the
morale and the reputation of teen-agers. Many newspapers have
teen pages or columns, cite teen-agers of the day, week or

month or hire teen columnists. The Buffalo (N.Y.) *Courier-Express* assigned a reporter to cover the positive side of teen-agers' lives, and his discoveries on this beat surprised both him and his editors. Wes Johns, describing his experience in *The Optimist* magazine, said that what he found in teen-age communities had been most refreshing. To him, the youngsters were an improvement on his own generation. This was especially true because of their strong sense of social consciousness, which he found to be much better developed than that of their elders. He concluded that teen-agers had been taken too much for granted and too often were classified either as good or bad, never as just average human beings.

With such kind words being said for teen-agers, it is well to ask, "Well, what *ARE* they doing that is so upbeat?"

Quite a bit, is the answer. Not so much as they might, but much more than many persons realize.

Doubters need only consider the examples that follow to be convinced that young people do more than steal automobiles, lounge in front of television sets, guzzle soda pop at drug stores or slouch around on street corners. The "pre-decents" keep busy, and without sociologists looking over their shoulders.

In Dickinson, Texas, a group of teen-agers have formed their own radio club, which they named "The Static Chasers." They participate in Civil Defense drills and serve as communications experts in hurricanes and other general disasters. With the help of the local Optimist Club, the youngsters set up headquarters in the basement of a fire house. When Hurricane Audrey of 1956 tore the antenna from the roof, the junior hams got the station back on the air so it could transmit emergency messages.

"The Static Chasers" have installed a public-address system in a Little League ball park and a two-way interphone hookup in the press box for football games at Gator Stadium. They now have a communications truck with field phones, a public-address system and a two-way radio, and they even have their own building.

Nearly 400 teen-agers belong to a social service club in St.

Louis County, Missouri, called Kennel City, U.S.A. They drew the name from the fact that the football team at Ritenour High School in Overland is known as the Huskies. Most of the club members attend Ritenour, but some are students at private and parochial schools. Kennel City operates on a city plan, with a mayor, councilmen, policemen and various other municipal titles. A "town meeting" is held every Wednesday night to plan projects such as taking orphans to baseball games or entertaining the monthly meeting of a Golden Age Club organized for persons over 70. In an Operation Alert, Kennel City sends its police force out to keep track of traffic violations by old and young alike. The teen-agers, in effect, police the police.

Mutual aid is the reason for an annual scholarship fund day at the Fort Lauderdale, Florida, High School, where each senior class member contributes his pay for a day's work. Grants totaling $30,000 have been made to deserving seniors through the performance of a variety of jobs. Girls work as service station attendants while boys serve as aides to police desk sergeants. Weeks before Work Day falls, the students canvass employers to arrange for jobs. The city hires seniors to clean streets and work in offices, and the FBI retains a student as "agent for a day." While earning money for their fund, the students also learn something of business, industry and city government.

Another mutual aid program was conducted at the Glen Cove High School on Long Island, where students in five French classes held benefits to raise nearly $1,000 so five classmates could study French during the summer. Fourteen teen-agers from Blaine County, Idaho, an isolated, mountainous sheep-and-cattle-raising area, labored nearly two years to help pay for tickets to Europe on their first trip to the "outside world." Fourteen boys and girls got jobs in sawmills, pitched hay, baked bread and performed various farm chores to finance the journey.

The interests of young people thus are as broad as the world and reflect what is going on in it.

When youngsters, with or without the aid of adults, decide it is "time for a project," the first thing they think of is likely to be a safety campaign, usually safety on the highways. The National Education Association encourages such programs in the schools; nearly 1,000,000 pupils in more than 1,000 schools have, in fact, joined the National Student Traffic Safety Program.

Some of the safety drives show considerable imagination. Students at the John Bartram High School in Philadelphia, for example, conducted test demonstrations at schools and industrial plants to help adult workers learn to be better drivers. A "conservation of human life" project was established at Union Springs Central School in Cayuga, New York, where teen-agers investigated the causes, times and places of accidents and the extent of the injuries that resulted. Their research led to a campaign urging drivers to obey the speed laws.

In their safety campaigns, youngsters often administer severe scoldings to adults. They get away with it, but there is little evidence that their "back-seat driving" instructions are heeded. Adults tend generally to keep teen-agers in the back seat in most activities. Young people are handy to have around when it is time to take up street- corner collections for polio, solicit home-owners for Red Cross contributions or scrub the municipal swimming pool. But the advice of the often inventive youngsters seldom is sought. That this is disappointing to the teen-agers is shown in a vote by Junior Achievement convention delegates, who gave a margin of almost two to one in favor of a suggestion that they should be included on the councils of civic groups.

One forward step has been taken in the schools, where student leaders are consulted by administrators on policies and plans for academic and extracurricular activities—and, wherever possible, the youthful suggestions are accepted. Sixty years ago there was almost no student government in high schools. Now, in many of them, student councils control activity budgets, produce assembly programs and monitor halls and lunchrooms. More than two-thirds of all American high schools have some form of student participation in school management. Students often are encouraged to expand their activities into their communities. This could help win them a place on civic councils, for if they go before adult groups as representatives of schools, they may receive more recognition than they would as individuals.

Another possible move toward broader acceptance of teen-agers as "young adults" can be detected in the development of teen-age codes in a number of communities. These frequently resolve into lists of "do's and don't's"—mainly "don't's"—for teen-agers, but sometimes they can create real adult-youth co-operation. In Bergen County, New Jersey, for example, the conduct of adults as well as children was subject to regulation in a behavior code. The rules grew out of a meeting called by bewildered parents seeking explanations of some of the teen-agers' wishes and demands. The Council of Jewish Women sponsored the project, forming a Family Relations Study Committee made up of Protestants, Catholics and Jews. A survey in which teen-agers participated showed that 95 per cent of them preferred to have their parents around at parties, but as "super-visors," not "snoopervisors." Ninety per cent of the youngsters said they opposed drinking and smoking.

A variety of codes has been drawn up for or by young people. Some deal with courtesy, others with good citizenship. Young people in Amherst, Massachusetts, wrote a code governing entertainment at home and on dates. One of the most inclusive codes, adopted at a conference of junior high school leaders from cities in northwestern Illinois, pleaded for acceptance of adolescents as working members of their communities so they could join in the fight against juvenile delinquency. Delegates wrote a code of conduct that covered dress, grooming, rules for dances and dates, smoking and drinking, dating and going steady, house parties, driving, jobs and curfews.

Another comprehensive code was prepared in Norwich, New York, under the sponsorship of the P-TA and with the leadership of a Norwich High School student, Weston G. Wickham. The Norwich Teen-Age Code Committee grew out of a joint interest in youth problems on the part of the Student Council and the P-TA.

"The youth of our vicinity had received a heavy barrage of

criticism in the local press and on radio," Wickham said. "We felt that our youth were certainly no worse than those of anywhere else, but perhaps we could improve youth and the public opinion of youth by setting up a 'code.'

"We formed a committee of three Student Council members and five P-TA members, plus alternates. We studied other codes. From these studies, we drew up questionnaires relating to youth. These questionnaires were sent to all seventh-through-twelfth-grade students and to everyone in the Norwich mailing district.

"Upon the compilation of these questionnaire replies and upon approval from the Student Council and the P-TA, we set up the Norwich youth-parent code, or 'teen-age code.' This code not only had do's and don't's for youth but also for parents."

The first recommendation in the "Social Code for Parents and Students" provides:

"Parents should encourage their children to bring their problems to them, listen to their opinions on matters which the teen-ager feels are important and resolve differences of opinion through open discussion."

The code holds parents responsible for the moral training and behavior of their children and for knowing at all times where and with whom their children are spending their leisure. "Parents and all adults working with young people should recognize their need for praise and readily give credit where credit is due," the family cooperation section recommends. Other clauses advise parents to provide wholesome recreation for children and assist in community projects for young people; to welcome their childrens' friends into their homes; to be present during parties and make sure no alcoholic beverages are served, and to set good examples as drivers.

Young people have responsibilities, too. The code recommends that children give their parents a chance to meet their friends and dates. Youngsters also should consult their parents before inviting friends into the house. Ten P.M. was agreed upon generally as the desired time for junior high school children to return home from dates on weekend nights. Midnight was the accepted curfew for senior high school students.

In an introduction addressed to students, parents and teachers, the P-TA pointed out that the nature and complexity of pressures on young people today would have amazed parents of two generations ago. Social customs have changed with the lessening of chaperonage, increased use of automobiles and more dates involving going out to movies, bowling alleys or dances instead of sitting in the parlor at home.

After observing the Norwich code in action for two years, Wickham commented:

"We feel that the code has provided a reference source for parents and students alike on youth questions and problems. We also feel that the code will serve as a guide for those students who are presently starting up the school climb."

The teen-age codes, if they accomplish nothing else, at least are making the adult community aware that there are young people who have other things on their minds besides vandalism, drinking and looting. They are part of the new look in J.D.— Juvenile Decency—of which there is a lot around, more than anyone knows. Statistics are kept on how many teen-agers are arrested on charges of stealing cars, burglarizing homes and inflicting bodily harm. These are easy to obtain. Whether they are an accurate reflection of the juvenile crime rate can be questioned with justification, for the figures are almost universally based on arrests rather than convictions.

There is no doubt that the stigma of the wrong kind of J.D. has made large numbers of innocent teen-agers guilty in the eyes of the public. It will take more than teen codes to remedy this unpleasant situation. Wider publicity could be given to the upbeat activities of the innocent youngsters, for they are deserving of more credit from their elders. Every local governing body might appoint a teen-age advisory council. The police could benefit, too, from the counsel of young persons. If a teenager is reliable enough to go out and collect funds for adult-run campaigns, he certainly is dependable enough to sit on the boards that organize those campaigns. And when the drives are over, adult leaders should be generous enough to acknowledge that they could not have done it without the stamina and spirit of their young assistants.

Ours is possibly the only culture in the history of civilization in which a person has not been considered "grown up" or expected to act "grown up" until he is old enough to vote. An arbitrary age has been set at which he suddenly becomes an adult. The teen-ager is segregated during the trying years in which he is not quite a "grown-up." Perhaps a little integration would go a long way toward bestowing equality on the young Americans, and as for where such integration should begin, there is no place like home.

.3.

Sex Is Not
a Four-Letter Word

Who told you the facts of life?

Almost certainly it was not your mother or father.

In all probability, your basic sex information came from someone your own age, a teen-age friend who took you aside and whispered about "s–e–x."

How much did you learn this way? Actually, not much. Basically you are ignorant about sex, no matter how much experience you may have had.

That has been the way of sex for generations.

Mass ignorance about the subject still exists in an era when SEX is thrown at young people from every direction. That ignorance is a result of the perennial failure by parents to perform what should be one of their most important jobs—teaching their children the facts of life, not just the biological facts, but the sociological, moral and psychological facts. Modern parents put on sophisticated fronts in cocktail party discussions of "those things," but when it comes to talking frankly with their children, many are almost as tongue-tied as their Victorian ancestors.

"Dear," a wife may say to her husband, "isn't it time you told Johnny *the facts?*"

"Oh," he replies, "he'll learn them anyway. Besides, I really don't know what to say. My father never told *me* anything, and I got along all right, so I guess he will, too."

22

The reluctance, or refusal, to tell Johnny and Jane about sex has forced most youngsters to continue to learn from each other, sometimes with disastrous results. That is what today's teenagers report when they are questioned individually and in the many surveys to which they are subjected. The results of a number of studies have shown that boys are even less likely than girls to be invited to have heart-to-heart talks with one parent or both.

Churches, schools and social agencies are at last trying desperately to fill the void traditionally left by the abdication of mothers and fathers. They do this despite opposition by some parents, who take the attitude that although *they* will not assume the responsibility themselves, it is no one else's business either. The institutional benefactors of the young are convinced there is no real substitute for responsible parental guidance, but they also feel that what they can do is better than nothing. Their desire is to give family-life counseling that is designed to encourage young people to regard sexual intercourse as part of a much larger area of life, not simply the physical and emotional gratification of the moment. They also are moving toward eliminating the old negative "sex is naughty" approach and replacing it with a positive interpretation of intercourse as an expression of conjugal love.

Sexual practices are being re-examined largely because in twentieth-century America reproduction no longer is the chief reason for intercourse, except among some religious groups. In past eras, couples produced as many offspring as they could, for they knew that disease, famine or war would kill most of them. Now, largely because infant and child mortality rates are low, the population has exploded, so the need is for *less* fertility and greater responsibility to society in planning children.

Young people today are maturing earlier than their parents did. They are dating, going steady, marrying and having babies at an earlier age. That means they are likely to have more, not fewer, children than their parents unless they are properly educated.

Teen-age marriages, many of them of the "shotgun" variety,

occur so frequently that they are hardly news any more. What *is* news is the teen-age divorce rate; girls 15 to 19 years old are getting more divorces than any other age group in the country. College students are marrying and starting families long before they get their degrees, but there has not been enough time yet to determine their divorce rate.

Many theories have been advanced on why youngsters are marrying at earlier ages. The foremost is that the girl is "in trouble." But why did she get that way? Some youngsters are forced into marriage because they have substituted experimentation for parental guidance. Some want to get married without realizing it, and having babies supplies them with an excuse, so they produce babies. Some are looking for affection wherever they can find it because they are not finding it at home. Some see the immoral example set by their elders and decide they might as well follow suit.

A noted psychologist was so concerned over the alarming rate of pre-marital intercourse in 1938 that he predicted that if the trend continued there would be no virgin brides in 1960. There have been increases in illegitimacy and teen-age marriages since 1938, but no one claims that there are *no* virgin brides, despite the artificial age limits for sexual activity imposed on young people by Western civilization. These restrictions ignore the fact that, biologically, humans are ready to copulate and reproduce long before society wants them to.

The limits are set without provision for constructive ways for young people to curb their natural desires or convincing reasons for them to do so. The once-convenient "scare" technique—babies and disease—no longer is effective, due to wonder drug treatments for venereal diseases and the development of easy-to-use contraceptives. Appeals for morality will have to be based on ethical and psychological grounds. A little sex education would go a long way, too, for today's young people are no better schooled in the subtleties of male-female relations than were their grandmothers.

Youngsters in the 1960's are *assumed* to know more about sex because they hear more about it on radio and television, see more of it in movies and advertisements and read more about it. Everyone is talking about sex these days. However, the parents of tomorrow cannot learn what they need to know about sexual intimacy from novels about adultery in suburbia, ads for "personal products" and Brigitte Bardot's often too generously exposed bosom. The combination of false modesty taught at home and false sexiness displayed in entertainment fare leaves youngsters confused and unenlightened.

Sex is used to stimulate business—sales of cigarettes, whisky, even breakfast food. Mothers tell children that sex is not a subject for polite society, and yet books, plays, movies, magazines, newspapers and even television glamorize it, often in the form of illicit indulgence. This is one double standard in sex. Another, about as old as Western civilization, allows men far more sexual freedom than women before society starts to frown. One reason for the large numbers of unwed mothers and forced marriages is a rebellion against this double standard. Girls are demanding equal rights—even to promiscuity and the risk of ruining their lives.

The scanty constructive information that is available to these youngsters is sought by progressively younger children. YWCA social workers, for example, used to channel most of their family-life material to women in their early twenties. Now teen-age girls and even pre-teens want to know what to expect of the marriage bed. A sixth grader's sister leaves the eleventh grade to get married and the younger child needs to know what it is all about.

This means that high school students are learning what colleges used to teach about sex and grammar school pupils want to know what formerly was taken up at the high school level. Parents contribute to the discussion principally to express fears that such indoctrination might lead to still earlier marriages, but it would seem that if a child knew early enough what was involved, the result would be less curiosity and experimentation and fewer early marriages.

Decreasing chaperonage and more familiarity among young-sters are other reasons for a greater need for them to know the facts of life and love sooner. Thirty years ago a well-brought-up girl did not remain in a parlor alone with a boy. Now all sorts of questions arise from the frequent trysts in automobiles, far from the safe atmosphere of the supervised settee.

A generation ago, a girl might have expressed her sexual con-cerns with such questions as, "Is it all right to French kiss?" "What about petting?" "What do I do to get a boy to like me if I'm not attractive?" "How far should I go to win his attention?" Today her questions seem more sophisticated, but she is just as ignorant, actually. She wants to know, "I want to marry this boy and he is a Catholic and I'm a Presbyterian—what about our children?" "Is it true you don't have to worry about venereal disease today with penicillin?"

A social worker who serves as a family-life counselor to girls in upper grades in grammar schools reported that she found sixth and seventh graders asking questions about Siamese twins and the inheritance of characteristics. They want to know about rape, and ask for details on how it is possible for a man to have his sex changed through surgery. These are things they have read about in newspapers and magazines.

Parents have been indicted widely and severely for their fail-ures as counselors. Frequently they react by passing the buck. They criticize schools because Johnny can't read, and they find fault with both church and school for his lack of knowledge about sex. "Let the church do it," they say. "Let the school do it." What they actually may be hinting at is that they themselves have learned little or nothing from the intimacies of marriage. Perhaps their abdication is a tacit admission that their own sex lives are inadequate, immature or without any real content. It is possible, too, that the failure of their parents to give guidance is being inflicted on the third generation.

Barriers have been built between parents and children that make youth and adults unable to talk with one another on a number of subjects. In one research study, boys and girls rated "petting" and "sex" as more difficult problems to discuss with their parents than any of thirty-six other possible topics. The result of this seems to be that young people are left to educate each other about sex.

The absence of help when it is needed is an almost open challenge to children to experiment with premarital relations during the time they are left too much on their own. The best some parents can do is to impose a curfew, limit the number of dates or try to find diversion for the children—to change the subject, so to speak. If they bothered to answer a few questions, the young people's preoccupation with the subject might not be so great.

"It is not because parents don't *want* to tell their children about the facts of life, but because they *don't know how,*" according to Mrs. Sara-Alyce Wright, teen-age program director of the National YWCA. "Parents of adolescents don't want to give their children evidence that they don't know what to do. They don't want to *feel* inadequate or give their children the idea that they *are* inadequate. They shift the subject elsewhere. Actually, a child's adolescence is one of the hardest periods for a parent to go through."

It also is a time for making mistakes. Parents often err in thinking that a large boy is grown up because he is big physically. He may have reached physical maturity, but emotionally he still is a child in a society that insists on twenty-one years of childhood. Even if he is the brightest boy in his class, it does not mean that he has emotional maturity. It is then that he needs help, but he may never ask for it—at least not at home.

There is a widely held theory that much of the trouble begins in the crib, when baby's exploratory investigations of his own body elicit horrified cries from his parents. Matters become worse in uneasy stages until the child eventually becomes reluctant to discuss anything sexual with his parents for fear it is "dirty."

"The average adult is so ashamed of sex, and so fearful of the sexual impulse, that he is hampered in any effort to be objective about it," declared Dr. Lester A. Kirkendall, author, counselor and professor of family life at Oregon State College, during one of the boldest dicussions of sex ever made public.

Kirkendall told 600 scientists, educators and clergymen brought together by the National Council of Churches and the Canadian Council of Churches in 1961 for a North American Conference on Church and Family Life that adults were afraid to display any real interest in sex for fear of adverse public opinion. The ubiquitous "they" might get the wrong idea.

"This fear has made it very difficult for us to communicate about sex or deal with it constructively," he said.

Another indictment came from Dr. Mary Steichen Calderone, medical director of the Planned Parenthood Federation of America, who told the meeting that most parents were emotionally unable to educate their children in sex.

"I think that the moment really has come when the churches must, to use an inelegant phrase, fish or cut bait," she said. ". . . Who really has a better right or a greater obligation to teach the details—the facts, the attitudes, the basic mores—about sex and its place in human life than the churches?"

The conference delegates openly discussed such once-taboo subjects as abortion, masturbation, homosexuality and infidelity. "Pregnant brides" was one extensively discussed topic in sessions devoted to matters that for years had been relegated to a kind of "underground." A set of recommendations was adopted urging the churches to help families adopt positive and realistic sex codes. It pleaded for the inclusion of sex education in Sunday schools on the theory that the philosophy of family planning must be taught from the youngest years just as much as reading, writing and arithmetic. Churches bless the sexual act in marriage, so why not make the preparation for this maturity complete with instruction in sex in Sunday school? It might produce a whole new generation of responsible parents.

As important as the recommendations themselves was the tone of the conference, which marked a departure from the traditionally sanctimonious church attitude toward sex. How long can the majority of the churches limit their stand to statements in favor of God and motherhood and against sin? That is what the churches are asking, at last. Some social workers feel that the church has more right to enter the field of sex education than does a social agency. But it must drop its "holy" approach in favor of being candid.

One of the more enlightened courses in family-life guidance has been introduced by the Protestant Episcopal Church under the title "Fit to Be Tied." It is a course for teen-agers giving them information without advice or preaching and enabling them to ask questions about anything they want to know. At introductory sessions held for them, parents have displayed eagerness for their children to receive such instruction. What is more, they often are worried lest their children's questions will not be answered forthrightly—this despite the fact that the parents will not answer the questions themselves.

In the series, youngsters are taught that physical cleanliness and neatness are related to sexual attraction. They are told that sex is "God-given" and provides both procreation and companionship. The young people submit anonymously the questions that they most want answered. Those asked with the greatest frequency cover such subjects as a girl's peak fertility period, artificial insemination, going steady, petting, masturbation, what a girl should do if a boy gets "fresh," homosexuality and birth-control devices. All are answered frankly and without sermonizing.

The Roman Catholic Church has had a sex-education program for many years. It stresses training in the home, by parents, with guidance from priests. This means that sex seminars are conducted for parents. They are informed that it is their obligation to educate their children in "the facts." Parents who are reluctant to do this or say that they do not know how to do it are persuaded to get up in class and explain sexual matters to each other as practice for talking to their children. They are admonished not to feel they must tell youngsters everything, however.

"Parents should talk to children, but there is no need to tell them every intimate detail," said the Very Reverend Monsignor George A. Kelly, director of the Family Life Bureau of the New York Archdiocese. "There should be something about the sex lives of parents that remains a secret between them."

While Father Kelly believes that sex has been overemphasized as an ingredient for a happy marriage, he also is convinced that it is more important to educate young people in "these matters" than it was thirty years ago.

"Silence then was not as harmful as silence now," he said. "In our culture, the influence of parents on children is minimal. Now parents are going to influence children again, but they have to be educated to do it."

Much of the sex education offered in Jewish community centers is on an informal basis involving small groups. Some centers hold classes for parents, as do the Catholics, to instruct them in how to deal with questions at home. Often a doctor or psychiatrist is called in to talk to a group. Young people are encouraged to go to center leaders when they have questions they do not feel they can ask their parents.

The YWCA has an up-to-date program of guidance in family planning. It offers courses to young girls and their mothers, and its field workers are always available to give counsel.

Sometimes the most helpful advice comes spontaneously during a social event or a club meeting, when a girl suddenly confronts a leader with a problem. This happened at a "Y" dance for teen-agers. One of the adult sponsors found it necessary to object to overly intimate dancing postures. She called the offenders to one side and talked with them quietly, explaining that they were not conducting themselves properly and warning them of the dangers in their behavior. Instead of being annoyed, the girls were grateful. Several sought out the adviser later and asked what they should do to keep boys from trying to make improper advances on the dance floor.

During the last few years, the "Y" has made a large and successful effort to alert young people to what life as adults is going to be like. One of the major segments of this program has been a series of meetings on family-life counseling. Actually, two almost identical series are held—one for mothers one day and the other for their daughters the next. This gives the mothers a chance to judge the programs and decide whether they want their girls to participate. It precludes any objections by mothers to the materials presented to adolescents. By keeping the girls segregated from their mothers, a freer atmosphere is created for the daughters to ask frank questions their mothers might worry over.

Many of the YWCA meetings feature movies, one on drinking, another on how much affection should be exchanged on dates. One of the more popular films shows a boy and a girl going home from a date. He makes a pass at her. The big question is, "What should she do?" They talk out the problem and part without kissing.

It has been suggested that schools are the ideal place—outside the home—for sex education, because almost every child turns up in a classroom. But there are pressures that restrict sexual teaching in the school—mainly from church groups and parents who challenge the right of the school to conduct such instruction. Many teachers, of course, are no better qualified to give sexual guidance than are parents. Some, indeed, are themselves the inadequate parents of questioning teen-agers. What the schools do present, therefore, often is sketchy, despite a joint effort by the National Education Association and the American Medical Association to introduce a series of teaching materials in the public school systems.

The cooperative effort has produced a series of booklets for parents and children delving into the basic questions asked by youngsters, how to answer them and what to do to prepare for marriage. Parents are told that the education of children in sexual practices should be regarded not as a task but as a privilege. The books go into considerable detail, with diagrams illustrating various physiological descriptions. It is a far more helpful series than the one it replaced, a sort of hearts and flowers set of pamphlets first published in the early 1930's.

Earlier discussions had such evasive titles as "Chums," "Margaret, the Doctor's Daughter," and "John's Vacation." They were uplifting discussions of the birds and the bees, but they were not very informative. These gave way to folksy discussions by a doctor, which in turn became dated and were replaced by the matter-of-fact booklets now being used.

Rarely is such material billed as "sex education." The term now is "family-life education." The main object of the change in emphasis has been to help youngsters see the relationship between sexual experience and the security of family life. An unmarried mother, for example, often gets "that way" because she did not understand what she was doing. Many young people know about the basic techniques of sex, but they have no idea of what they really mean. They know the biological facts, but not in terms of their own bodies—at least, not until it is too late. Teen-agers tend to put on sophisticated fronts indicating that they *know everything,* but this is a cover-up, possibly as much so as the pseudosophistication of their parents.

Here are some remedies:

—When a parent does not know the answer to a problem, he or she should admit it and say to a child, "I don't know, but let's try to find the answer together." This would put them on an equal footing and give them something basic to talk about.

—Courses in sex education should be offered widely to parents so they can teach their children themselves. By discussing their difficulties with other parents and with counselors, they might lose some of their inhibitions. It might also be possible for them to grow along with their children.

—Sunday school curriculum materials should include graded courses in sex education so complete that when a child reaches puberty he will have learned the basic facts in church. Some advocates of such a program say that the meanings of terms such as prostitution, abortion, venereal disease and homosexuality should be taught in Sunday school.

—Church, school, social agency and parents need to reappraise sex standards to de-emphasize concern over the sexual act itself and put new emphasis on the sexual relationship as a symbol of the quality of the whole relationship between two persons.

—The churches should drop traditional approaches to sex and seek real teamwork with doctors and psychiatrists.

—Parents should abandon scare techniques in instilling morality. Adults should, rather, talk to teen-agers in terms of their own futures and those of *their* children.

A small beginning has been made. It is hoped that much more will be accomplished. But parents must emerge from their prolonged adolescent attitudes toward love and marriage if Johnny and Jane are to be convinced that sex really is not a four-letter word.

.4.

Preventive Engagement

—Engagement Terminated—

Mr. and Mrs. John S_____ announce the termination of the engagement of their daughter, Jane, to Mr. Thomas J_____ Jr., son of Mr. and Mrs. J_____. The marriage had been scheduled for Aug. 2. The engagement was terminated by mutual consent.

THAT NEWS ITEM, CONTRARY TO WHAT THE TOWN GOSSIPS SAID, told of a successful engagement, not a broken one. It was successful because it prevented a failure—a divorce.

Both Jane and Tom were winners because they found out before it was too late that marriage would have been a mistake for them—*and they were willing to admit it.* They had put to use, intentionally or not, one of the most startling new weapons offered for the war against divorce—the preventive engagement.

Instead of squandering their engagement on exchanging blissful glances and holding hands at parties given in their honor, they went through a trial period, taking long walks and drives, having intense talks on what they believed and did not believe and what they thought they wanted out of life. They delved into one another's interests, religious leanings, attitudes toward children and favorite leisure-time activities. She saw him when he needed a shave and he had a good look at her in hair curlers and without lipstick. He managed to eat a dinner she had

34

cooked. She had a chance to observe his behavior with their friends' children. They went shopping together, for clothes, groceries, books and phonograph records. And they had more than their quota of quarrels.

What they found out was that after the honeymoon had ended they would have had nothing much to talk about and little to build upon for the rest of their lives. Marriage, for them, simply would not have worked, so they took advantage of the escape clause that should be part of every engagement.

The thing that happened to Jane and Tom is regarded by society as a broken engagement. About half of all formal engagements end that way. Many more should, judging from the number that lead to marriages that are flops from the moment the strains of the Wedding March have faded away.

Teen-age elopements have increased sharply and so has the teen-age divorce rate, but a hopeful sign is found in the trial engagement. Couples who recognize their incompatibility short of the altar are sparing themselves not only the possible ordeal of divorce, but perhaps something worse, a disaster that is one of the chief causes of heartache in America today. It is called married misery, and it strikes possibly 20 out of every 100 homes.

Surveys have produced estimates that about 50 per cent of the divorcing couples in the United States have been married no more than five years. Twenty-five per cent have been married less than two years. Trial engagements might have helped prevent such calamities by averting the marriages in the first place.

"I'm much more worried about the number of unhappy marriages than about the divorce rate," says the Reverend Dr. Everett C. Parker, director of communications of the United Church of Christ and a specialist in trying to steady rocky marriages. "The vast majority of people who get married stay married, but far too many of them are unhappy together and need help."

The Reverend Oscar E. Feucht of the adult education department of the Lutheran Church-Missouri Synod says that the misery in marriage is as serious a problem as actual divorce.

"Thousands of couples live in armed truce or in almost unbearable anguish of heart," he says. "They refrain from divorce out of one or more of the following considerations: children, property, business, need of support, moral or religious reasons, fear of publicity and inability to pay the court costs. When we take these unsuccessful marriages into consideration, we see how large our problem at its base really is."

Where does the blame lie? Sometimes hasty marriages are at fault. In others, youth and inexperience are the twin culprits. There is a chance most of the misery could have been obviated by preventive engagements.

"All marriage failures are courtship failures," says William Genné, head of the family-life department of the Division of Christian Education of the National Council of Churches and one of those who holds that quite a few engagements exist only to be broken. "Many couples don't use their courtships wisely. They are underrated. Often a courtship is just a round of parties, getting ready for the marriage ceremony instead of the marriage."

Every engaged couple needs a few sharp jolts to reveal faults as well as fancies. One of the best eye-openers is a quarrel, but, unfortunately, too few persons know how to have a good spat and get it settled without leaving scars that never will heal. Many men and women simply do not know how to have a disagreement, never having seen two adults have an honest difference of opinion and work it out. Parents usually stop a quarrel among children just to silence the noise. They do not take the trouble to teach the youngsters how to settle their differences. As a result, when the children grow up and have a quarrel, they do not know what to do.

There are many young people who try to take marriage seriously, despite the wave of teen-age marriages—many of them out of necessity. Increasing numbers of persons are enrolling in premarital counseling courses in colleges and seeking help from various advisers. Some are turning to preliminary investigatory relationships of their own even before committing themselves to formal engagements. "Going steady," wearing a fraternity pin and other rituals of young love can be important preludes to an engagement, often eliminating the need for the skills of a marriage counselor.

When the mothers of the upbeat generation were dancing the Big Apple back in the 1930's, the degree of a bobby-soxer's popularity was measured not only by the number of dates she had each week but by the number of boys who courted her company. Going steady was mainly for the less popular girls, then frequently called "drips." Being seen at every dance and picnic with the same fuzzy-cheeked boy often was considered a social stigma, although it still was an improvement over staying at home. Today if a girl, whether beauty or beatnik, does not go steady, she is considered something of a "dog" or "pretty far out." The other girls conclude that she really does not have what it takes to interest one young man for long.

In the interval since the fickle 1930's and 1940's there has evolved an elaborate courtship system mixing elements of sentimentality, economy and tribalism. It could be called romance on the installment plan, and it is related to the new preventive engagement.

Beginning with going steady and exchanging slave bracelets in grade school and ending at the altar, young people have developed a series of romantic rituals that require boys to finance an almost constant outpouring of gifts for their girls, in return for which the boys appear to achieve the status of superbuyers, if not supermen.

The step-by-step progression in the development of romantic sophistication goes something like this:

Going steady: A friendship ring or slave bracelet often is presented by a boy to a girl with whom he goes steady in high school— or even in grade school. This is his notice to other boys to stay away from his "private property." It is the girl's "social security." It is a guarantee of a date every Saturday night. Boys and girls feel popular if they have this date insurance, despite the fact that each goes out with only one person.

Lavaliering: In college, or perhaps the final year of high school, a boy may present his girl with a lavalier, which is a chain from which his gold football, fraternity insignia or club emblem dangles. This means that they think they are *more* than going steady—a term frowned on as childish by many college students nowadays—but actually they are no more committed than if they were, in fact, going steady.

Pinning: The gift of a fraternity pin from a boy to a girl usually is looked upon by the couple as "being engaged to be engaged," a period in which young people can be in love and think about matrimony without getting their parents involved in the intricacies of a formal engagement. Some couples go straight from pinning to marriage, so it can be an actual engagement. But most who pass through this stage eventually send out announcements. The pinning ritual itself can be mystical, with ceremonies involving candles, the reading of poetry and, finally, the "sacrifice" of the "pinned" pair—not on flaming pyres but in ice-cold water.

Watching: At any time during the pinning period, a girl may be "watched"—literally. It means she is given a wrist watch as a present. It *can* mean that she is a tiny step nearer the altar but it also can indicate nothing more than that the boy wants to give her something; it gives him self-confidence to do so. Gifts of value are an important aspect of modern courtship, while in Grandma's day, social practices pretty much limited a boy to bestowing only edible presents, mainly candy. It is important to a boy today to have people know he can buy an expensive gift for his girl. And it means even more to many a girl to be able to say, "George bought me this watch."

Becoming engaged: If a couple has been through any preliminary steps, the engagement probably is a short one, possibly lasting only a few weeks. If the early rituals have been ignored, the engagement could last years. Those who go in for pinning and all the other accompaniments to love on the campus regard the standard formal engagement as something mainly for parents—a time for *them* to enjoy the social status that goes with pictures in newspapers, articles describing pedigrees, parties and other frills.

This system of romance on the installment plan rarely results in the marriage of the same two persons who exchanged slave bracelets on their way home from seventh grade. Many young- sters go steady two, three or four times before they have finished high school. But they learn about the opposite sex in these five easy stages, and largely without much parental help or supervision.

Some time after World War I, parents decided chaperonage and other close supervision were old-fashioned. More and more through the decades, the so-called "progressive" parents have left young people to their own resources. As a result, young people have built up their own code of social behavior. They took over the adult practice of pairing off in rebellion against the rat-race of popularity. Gradually today's gingerly progression developed.

There are some young people who mistakenly think that under this elaborate ritual they are almost irrevocably committed by the time the engraved engagement announcements have been mailed and their parents have gone into conference with the caterers. Many parents regard engagements as so binding that their sons and daughters leave the engagement until just before the wedding. It is much easier to return a pin, a gold football or a slave bracelet than a diamond engagement ring.

Girls take varying views of "pinning." Some do not want a pin without a promise of marriage. Others *collect* fraternity pins. (A few boys have been known to invest in several pins, but this is a secret between them and the makers of fraternity insignia.)

As soon as a girl is "pinned," the collegiate rituals begin. Little attention is paid to the bestowal of slave bracelets, lavaliers or watches, but pinning is a big event. The tribal customs surrounding pinning differ in various parts of the country and from campus to campus. Some students spurn the practice as "sophomoric." "We believe in all or nothing," a young Princetonian said. "An engagement ring or nothing at all. The rest is pretty high-schoolish."

At Northwestern University, near Chicago, pinning is regarded by many sorority girls as a bigger event than an engagement. The ring merely confirms an agreement to marry. When a boy gives a girl his fraternity pin, however, the recipient's sorority goes into a kind of seance at which the members stand in the dark in a circle while the housemother passes a lighted candle from girl to girl. When the candle reaches the girl who has been pinned, she blows out the flame, thus announcing that she is the lucky one.

After the cries and squeals of delight have died away, the girl's sorority sisters seize upon her and drag her fully-clad to the nearest shower and thrust her under a stream of cold water. Why? No one seems to know.

A little later, the fraternity whose member has "pinned" the now soaked and bedraggled girl gathers outside the sorority house and serenades all the members. Then the boys drag their hero of the moment to the shores of Lake Michigan and throw him in, even if they have to break the ice to do it.

At the University of Missouri, after a boy has "pinned" a girl, he is invited to dinner at her sorority house. Then his fraternity invites the girl to dinner. When the fraternity appears to serenade the sorority, it presents a large box of candy to the housemother, who passes it around. The "pinned" girl gets a bouquet of roses. After the serenade, the sorority sisters respond with a special song of their own.

In at least one sorority on the Missouri campus, when the senior members sit down for their last breakfast, each one who is neither engaged nor pinned is required to eat a lemon. "It was shocking," a recent graduate said, "to see how many girls got pinned or engaged just to avoid the lemon torture."

Similar practices were reported on other campuses, with students almost universally looking upon "pinning" as "being engaged to be engaged" but not necessarily leading to a formal engagement.

At the University of Michigan, when a co-ed becomes engaged, she puts a lighted candle in her window and her fiancé's fraternity serenades her. If a Sigma Chi is the fortunate one, his fraternity brothers burn a large paper heart while they sing "Sweetheart of Sigma Chi."

Far Western students have their variations on the same theme, with the basic ingredients still candles, candy, serenades, flowers —and cold water, more often in pitchers, however, than in lakes.

One of the worst mistakes an adult can make is to laugh at any of this. Nearly every young person involved in such rites goes through them solemnly and sincerely.

"I find that this generation does not hand out pins in the profusion in which our generation did, and they take it very seriously," says Herbert N. Heston, speaking both as director of the office of development of Smith College and as a father. "Any parent who takes this too lightly in front of the youngster involved is asking for trouble."

The anthropologist Ashley Montagu takes a harsh view of pinning as "an absurd tribalism—evidence of false values. Going steady in my view is an evidence of insecurity and also what goes with immaturity and conformity. It is insecurity in the sense that once you've cottoned onto someone you hang on for fear you might not cotton onto someone else. You need experience before you are a mature human being. It is much wiser to share experience with all kinds of people.

"Going steady and pinning are part of conformity, a wrong sense of values. Fraternity pins are like one of these things the African native in the jungle pins on a subject and says, 'This is my property, keep off.' It has no quality behind it.

"There is no objection to anyone's developing a strong affection for one person at the college level. But most intelligent students don't get involved. The brightest and best-rounded say, 'I'm really here to study, not to get married.' "

Montagu's view is shared by few. Actually the progressions and rituals he regards as absurd tribalism can be part of preventive engagement, the value of which certainly cannot be ridiculed with any justification. Any trial period should involve a couple's putting themselves into as wide a range of circumstances as possible—and then as objectively as possible discussing the results. If after they have finished their self-prescribed paces they think of themselves as a couple and not individuals, they may be on the right road together.

This does not mean an engagement should be just one long, marathon game of Twenty Questions, with the prize being the kiss at the altar. But it does mean that a girl and boy should decide to accept one another as each is before marriage instead of devoting the engagement period to charting blueprints for making changes, each in the other, after the wedding. Some girls commit romantic suicide by turning managerial as soon as they get their engagement rings, which implies that they have not learned much from love—at least they have not found out that you cannot teach a young dog new tricks any more than you can teach them to do an old one.

Dr. Abraham Franzblau, psychiatrist and teacher of marriage counseling courses, joins some young people in having mixed feelings about training for domesticity. He says "a good marriage is not made by a six-month course in college or by a few lectures by a minister in the weeks before the ceremony or in the engagement period. The correction of mistakes and understanding of what is involved in marriage is something that takes a lot of doing. Marriage is one of the most difficult things in the human experience. It takes the highest effort, not six lessons from Madame La Zonga."

"Experts" in the field of marriage generally agree that the younger the couple, the longer the engagement should be and the greater the emphasis on misery prevention. They also hold that the more thorough the preparation, the more solid the start of the marriage and the less strife there will be later.

Montagu believes in the "durable" engagement—"I'd give it a year. If there are doubts at the end of a year, a couple should take a vacation. The engagement should be a period of getting to know each other and going through the *Sturm und Drang* of little disagreements and things that rub the wrong way. It should be a period for discovering each other and ironing out all those things. In our society, we get married and then try to iron things out. That's why one out of three marriages ends in divorce."

Others place stress on maturity, with the degree of maturity not always dependent on the ages of those involved. A "mature couple" according to the Reverend Leslie Conrad Jr., a United Lutheran pastor and executive secretary of the Luther League, is "two persons who have surveyed the opposite-sex field, and find each other to be the pick of the lot; they are wise enough to spend considerable time with their respective circle of friends, and a sensibly proportioned amount of time with each other; they have plenty of other-than-each-other interests to involve them, such as school and church clubs and organizations; they are so well grounded in principles that premarital intercourse is recognized by both as 'no trespassing' territory."

Those who counsel couples on their personal lives are aware that the divorce rate continues to rise no matter what they say or do. But they have hope for the more recently married young people who have taken the trouble to try to prepare for the fact that love *must* come in the door when romance flies out the window. Time is the key. If a marriage survives the first ten years, the second critical period is most likely to come after the children are grown—and often after years and years of married misery.

It is because of such misery that the Roman Catholics have an active program for urging constructive use of the engagement. The Right Reverend Monsignor Irving A. de Blanc, director of the Family Life Bureau of the National Catholic Welfare Conference, tells young Catholics that in many ways the engagement period is the most important aspect of marriage. "It is," he says, "a period of learning to know each other well, of getting used to being a couple, of planning ahead for marriage, of being sure you are both prepared to unite until death. It is not a time to be spent mainly in making the rounds of exhausting parties, of going on hectic shopping trips or of becoming overly concerned with petty details.

"Stepping into an airplane does not make one a pilot, nor does putting on a wedding band make a real husband or wife. There is much more to it than spending a few minutes at the altar. Brides, for instance, should know before they are married much more than how to use a can opener or how to manage frozen foods."

De Blanc says that a girl must take into marriage with her

a fund of knowledge about homemaking as broad and substantial as the knowledge her husband will use in earning money to run the home. "He shows his love for his wife by being a good machinist, accountant, salesman or doctor," he said. "She should show her love by being a good cook, housekeeper and mother."

One of the most important rules, as far as Monsignor de Blanc is concerned, is: "Expect many changes of mind—even about marrying each other. If you are not reasonably sure of each other, then investigate it thoroughly while you are only engaged and not married."

Dr. Olin T. Binkley, dean of the faculty of Southeastern Baptist Theological Seminary, also advocates the availability of an easy exit from every engagement. "One of the purposes of the engagement in our culture," he says, "is to test the wisdom of the tentative choice of mates. I am convinced that it is appropriate for the man and woman in courtship to treat each other as whole persons and not as sexual beings only, and that it is helpful for them to speak the truth to one another. The engagement provides an opportunity for man and woman to reveal their minds to one another and to learn to trust one another. This pattern of communication formed in courtship may be continued in marriage. Unfortunately, mechanisms of deception used in courtship sometimes reappear in marriage and damage the dynamic inter-personal relationship of husband and wife."

Dr. Harry F. Tashman, a well-known psychoanalyst who specializes in marital problems, believes that a couple should use the engagement period for a "sensible investigation—a trial-and-error period. They should study the families of each other, look over the parents. An apple doesn't fall far from the tree. The individual may resemble one of his parents. That gives an idea of what he may be like. The idea of an engagement is that a person who gets out of it may be succeeding at something. An engagement is a sort of commitment, but if an individual has any sense of honor, justice or reliability, he should break it if he thinks he has made a mistake."

What is the prescription for preventive engagement? There are a number of measures young people can take to test themselves. Here is one recommended dosage:

1. Spend a week living with your prospective in-laws, not just as a social visit but by joining in their everyday life. This should give a rough idea of what life with their child might be like.

2. Go to concerts, play golf, take hikes, go for long drives or do whatever interests both or either of you but do it alone together, to determine whether you have interests in common or will not object to each other's interests.

3. Introduce each other to the friends you knew before you met. Have parties at which they are included, along with the acquaintances you have made together since your romance began. How they mix and how both of you mix with all of them should give some interesting insights.

4. Try to find a way to introduce each other to the boys and girls you have gone with in the past—or at least one in whom you were romantically interested. If this cannot be arranged, at least discuss past romantic involvements. Reactions to such disclosures can bring out signs of a jealous nature.

5. Either go to church together or discuss religion at length, including whether you plan to enter religious activities after marriage and whether your children will be reared in a religion.

6. Spend as much time as possible with children, to see how you both get along with them. Then decide whether you want children of your own, and, if so, how many. Also discuss the possibility of adoption, if for any reason you doubt that you can have children.

7. Have the bride-to-be cook a few meals for her fiancé, to show him her degree of skill in the kitchen. He, in turn, should demonstrate that he is able and willing to earn a living.

8. Spend a lot of time together doing nothing in particular, talking when you feel like it and remaining silent when you

wish. If the silences are uncomfortable, you may be in trouble.

9. Criticize each other's shortcomings—constructively—but admit from the outset that there is no hope of reforming a person by marrying him. Decide whether you are willing to accept each other just about as you are.

10. Go shopping together. Much can be learned about a person by observing whether he is a careful shopper or an extravagant one, how he treats sales people and if he can make up his mind.

These "pills" are refinements of the wisdom of experts in the marriage field. If they are easy to swallow, the next step may be the altar and a happy marriage. But if they are bitter, do not feel you have failed. The engagement still will have been successful—by preventing married misery.

.5.

You Need Not Be a Football Hero...

No ONE IS CERTAIN EXACTLY WHERE OR WHEN IT HAPPENED, whether at a street corner apple stand, beside a WPA ditch-digging project, or at Pearl Harbor, Anzio or Omaha Beach, but death struck down Joe College—banjo-strumming, booze-drinking flivver driver and dedicated *C* student—some time between the last riotous three-day college weekend house party of 1930 and the enrollment of the first World War II veteran under the G.I. Bill of Rights. Joe College, with his social snobbery, raccoon coat and hip-pocket flask, may have died a hero, but he goes unmourned by a new generation of college students who embody the unlikely combinations of conformity and individualism and of studiousness and protest, who sport Phi Beta Kappa keys rather than beanies and who hang diapers on the housing project clothesline instead of tacking-up pennants in a fraternity house.

Betty Co-ed, who grew out of flapperhood into permanent adolescence with the notion that knowing how to Charleston was more desirable than a bachelor's degree, joined Joe College in merciful eclipse. She turns up sometimes at costume parties, in short skirt and silk stockings rolled to the knee, but no one takes her seriously now just as no one did then. The Jazz Age college girl who went along for the tin lizzie ride with the "rah-rah" boy is likely to be the bored grandmother of a bespectacled young woman who hopes for a career as an astro-physicist and whose knowledge of life almost certainly does not include the adventures of Harold Teen. That young woman is as unlikely to know about autographed slickers as about rumble seats and may think the gearshift rod was invented for the sports car she wheedled out of her father as a high school graduation gift. But she is developing resources that will enable her, forty years from now, to elude the boredom that has en-gulfed her ex-flapper grandma.

Gone with Joe College and Betty Co-ed are the sentiments made popular by the song that said you had to be a football hero to get along with a beautiful girl. You don't have to be a football hero any more. In fact, it is just as well if you are not. The hero of today's college girl keeps his nose in a book much of the time, and when he does participate in a sport, it is likely to be for fun, not for a letter ten inches high to wear on his chest. He is more likely to spend his time in the labora-tory or at lectures or demonstrating against social injustice than either cheering himself hoarse over a football game or playing in it.

Old grads often express astonishment at what they see when they return to their alma maters for class reunions. It is no wonder, for the so-called country club colleges of the days when bathtubs were for gin and mink was for football have become educational factories, turning out young people schooled with such efficiency—and often impersonality—that they attend classes by the remote control facility of television and are one step from having their courses planned for them by IBM cards.

The college students of the 1920's and possibly even the 1930's were such stereotypes that they were sitting targets for cartoonists and lampoonists. Today it is impossible to depict the campus species in the way John Held Jr. did in his famous cartoons. It has been tried, but without success. Colleges and universities are diverse now, and so are the students. Earlier in the century, a typical undergraduate went to college to major in drinking, singing and cheering for the football team; for the prestige of being able to say, "Well, when *I* was in college," and, incidentally, for some book learning. He wanted to be a member of America's "élite educated class." A college diploma was a passport to "success," but it was embarrassing to get grades higher than a *C;* anyone who did was regarded as a "greasy grind"—the rough equivalent of today's "square" or "gnerd." This is not to say that there were no real students, for there always is some cream that rises to the top, but the bookworms were out of step with Joe College, the king of the campus.

The stereotype persisted for years. It had vanished by the time the end of World War II set off an invasion of education-hungry veterans onto college campuses, taking their wives and babies with them. The sons of poorly educated laborers found acceptance at the best of colleges, and members of every religion and race engaged in higher studies on the basis of brain power, not skin color or belief. The rich man's son found himself in a minority among men and women working their way through college or studying on scholarships. Being a Phi Beta Kappa became something even heirs to fortunes could be proud of, and doctorates elicited envy rather than scorn.

After the first post-war burst of enthusiasm, a certain degree of apathy pervaded campuses, due in part to the Korean War and in part to Senator McCarthy's mass intimidation of youth. Cynicism and a kind of emptiness set in. The Spirit of Old Siwash of the 1920's was only a legend. The radical movements of pre-World War II days were but memories. Then, slowly, a new spirit arose. The student emerged from himself. A crack developed in the ivory tower and light from the outside world poured in. The student began dressing more conventionally and making forays off campus. He found himself equally at home in the city, in the suburb, with his family and at school. He was more likely to drink, but in smaller quantities than his father before him. College newspapers began reporting

more of the serious events on campuses—and news of the world
—and less of the hullaballoo.

F. Scott Fitzgerald and his drunken wading parties in the
fountain in front of New York's Plaza Hotel nearly were laid
to rest in the fall of 1961 when a bold young editor announced
the demise of *The Princeton Tiger,* famous humor magazine
published by Princeton undergraduates, and its replacement
with a publication catering to students more sophisticated than
those of the 1920's. Startled alumni and trustees acted in the
emergency. They preserved the venerable magazine by remov-
ing the editors who found themselves unable to laugh at their
grandfathers' corny jokes.

The maturity—call it sophistication if you like—being mani-
fested on most campuses is due in large part to the enormous
growth of universities in or near big cities. Another reason is
that college students, on the average, are older than they were
twenty years ago, and increasing numbers have decided in their
freshman year that they will take graduate work. More of them
report for freshman orientation week already set on a career,
whereas a generation ago college often was regarded as "a good
place to grow up, to mark time," until a person had decided
what he wanted to make of his life. There is too much to learn
and too much emphasis on specialization today for a young
person to lapse into the luxury of that kind of college career.
Schools have become tougher, both to get into and to stay in.
Employers want trained college graduates to work for them and
care less about their undergraduate clubs than about their
courses.

Whether the new student is a cause or a result, he leaves
college rated as brighter, better-educated, better-informed, more
mature and harder-driving than members of previous generations. So intent on education is he that on some campuses it
is difficult to find students to serve as leaders. They do not have
time for extraneous matters. Being a Big Man on Campus
simply does not have the appeal of former years.

There is less adherence to college tradition and campus spirit as a result. The graduate of 1962 is far less likely to return to class reunions than the graduate of 1932; he finds it more important to cement a few close personal relationships than to be part of an "inseparable" group. Students turn up in larger numbers at campus lectures and concerts than at class proms, which are going into gradual eclipse.

Every year since World War II, there have been fewer big proms and less interest in those that have been held. Students prefer small, informal parties with music on hi-fi or by a local combo—dances at which everyone knows everyone else and the dress is informal. At New York University, fifty couples out of a possible 600 attended what was billed as a Gala Prom. Only 300 couples out of a class of 3,000 turned up at a big UCLA dance. Michigan dropped its famous J-Hop, once the major social event of the year for the entire town of Ann Arbor. There have been no proms for several years at Beloit College, in Wisconsin, and the University of Texas. Perhaps this is a reflection of the pattern of adult socializing, which also has become more easygoing, more intimate and, in many cases, less costly.

If all the students eligible were to turn out for proms at many schools, there would not be halls large enough to hold them. Campuses are overflowing with students and the inundation increases every year. There were 6,000,000 college graduates in the population in 1950 and 8,000,000 in 1960. The figure is expected to rise to 11,000,000 by 1970 and to 15,000,000 by 1980.

College students and graduates obviously make up a relatively small proportion of the total population, but they are the wellspring of the nation's leadership on nearly every level and in nearly every kind of endeavor. Schools have been expanding rapidly and new ones have been organized. The boom in higher education has brought the development of more large universities and a greater degree of conformity on the part of the individual student, but with less of an "organization" approach. Students tend to accept social decrees without protest, although they may prefer not to be members of a rigid social group. On many campuses they dress much the same as the rest of society, except perhaps in the relatively isolated colleges such as Vassar, where girls are inclined to slop around in blue jeans during the week and primp on Saturdays for dates with boys from Yale and other near-by men's schools.

Colleges and universities generally used to ban married students from campuses. Now, however, about 25 per cent of all students are married, most of them in the older age bracket. Some of the married students attend only part-time while holding full-time jobs, which are far more plentiful than in former days. Special housing is provided for married students on some campuses, most notably the University of California at Berkeley, which has provided apartments for couples—often to the consternation of single students, who also would like to abandon dormitory living for the comforts of a more homelike atmosphere.

The need to work while attending school is greater, not smaller, despite prosperity. The cost of higher education has become inflated beyond the bank accounts of even relatively prosperous parents, so the student who is working his way through college is not an oddity any more.

School officials appear to agree generally that more students are coming from "working class" homes—lower-middle and lower income groups. That is one reason why there has been a serious decline in the quality of students' spelling and grammar.

The undergraduate is ambitious and he also is restless. Transfers from college to college are becoming more frequent. Instead of being miserable, young people are willing to admit they made a mistake and seek to finish elsewhere. New York University, for example, has found that there is no place like home as far as students from the big city are concerned. NYU officials report that an astonishing number of New Yorkers who go away to college cannot wait four years to return. Other

chools have discovered the same thing, with the result that a
.ind of educational game of musical chairs has resulted. One
najor step has been from girls' or boys' schools to coeducational
nstitutions. Another has been from "cow colleges" to big-city
iniversities.

Some educators are awakening to the realization that the
lay of sexually segregated schools may be nearing an end be-
:ause it is contrary to the modern mores of American society.
)r. Sarah Gibson Blanding, president of Vassar, sounded a
'eminist alarm in a speech declaring that within the next
wenty-five years many of the 100 women's colleges would cease
o exist as they are and that no more than ten would be operat-
'ng at the end of the next century. She believes some will be-
:ome affiliated with universities, a move that would put them
in the coeducational sphere, while others will open their class-
:ooms to men and become completely coeducational. Another
ilternative she presented was that the government would take
)ver some women's schools.

Barriers had been falling before Dr. Blanding spoke. Barnard
College girls were sharing professors and classrooms with
Columbia College students. Radcliffe and Harvard had been
growing increasingly integrated. Yale admitted some women
students. Hunter College in New York, once a girls' school,
now is completely coeducational. Princeton accepted its first
woman student in 1961—in its graduate school—which is where
sexual integration often begins in men's colleges.

The elimination of waste is the chief reason for this kind
of integration. Many college facilities are not being used efficiently. There is duplication of faculty efforts, a problem that
is being overcome by a group of small Western New York
colleges, which are banding together for an interchange of
teachers and coordination of administrative procedures. There
is an arbitrary limit on academic life to a thirty-five-hour week
—seven hours five days a week—and, on many campuses, to
eight months a year. Dr. Blanding said that if women's colleges
were to survive as they are—and her comments hold true for

many other schools, too—they would have to use plant facilitie and faculty time more efficiently.

It is possible, although she did not say so, that women' colleges have outlived their usefulness. They were establishe in a day when existing colleges and universities were close to women and women did not have the vote. The college woman was an oddity and likely to face a life of spinsterhood Now women are accepted generally on an equal footing with men. The woman college graduate is almost as certain to marry as any other woman. Those loyal to feminine bastions o higher education maintain that women need a different kind o education than men, but this theory is questionable in an era when coal mines are about the only places of employment stil closed to women, and, one would hope, permanently so.

Schools once exclusively male preserves have accepted women more readily than women's schools have admitted men. This resulted in a rise in the enrollment of women in the fall o 1961 to 37.8 per cent of the total college and university popula tion. Men accounted for 68.3 per cent in 1960 and dropped tc 62.2 per cent of the 3,891,000 enrolled for the 1961-62 school year. Most of the increase in women students was reported by coeducational schools or institutions once exclusively for men which have more to offer women seeking professional training. A girl who wants to become an engineer is not likely to enroll in Wellesley, for example. Some Vassar graduates go on to co educational medical schools but most girls seeking medical degrees prefer to do their undergraduate work in the company of men.

No one has forecast the end of all-male campuses as Dr. Blanding has of the women's schools, but the end is coming nevertheless. One-time masculine sanctuaries seem to have withstood the shock of the feminine presence with a minimum of protest, possibly because they have adopted a policy of gradualism but also doubtless because men have by now become so inured to the infiltration of women that one more incursion is of little import.

Radcliffe has managed to become partly integrated with Harvard and, at the same time, to retain its identity, and perhaps this will be the pattern followed by other schools. In the belief that women have some educational problems not confronted by men, Radcliffe has established a new Institute for Independent Study, which provides a program of graduate courses for women who married and reared children after college and now find themselves too rusty to resume careers. Mrs. Mary I. Bunting, Radcliffe's president, introduced the program out of concern over "the luxurious ambiguity" of the educated woman of today. So great is the need for educated persons in specialized fields that she considers it a near-disastrous waste when domesticity removes a woman from the talent pool and makes her an intellectually displaced person.

The Radcliffe program, which Mrs. Bunting hopes will be copied elsewhere, provides for a nucleus of twenty gifted women to work as part-time scholars on $3,000 grants for a year of study in art, writing, history, science, social science, creative art and other subjects. They are talented women whose careers have been interrupted and who cannot resume them without new intellectual stimulation. Named also are resident fellows, distinguished women to work on long-range programs for five years, with stipends of $10,000 a year each.

Mrs. Bunting's program emphasizes independent study, which is being developed on a number of campuses as a movement away from "spoon-feeding" students, away from "packaged education" with quotas of credits and hours, rigid reading programs and uniform examinations.

Many experiments are being conducted in the realm of independent reading or research, with teacher participation limited to guidance. Oberlin, for example, has been turning freshmen loose to explore mathematics, zoology and psychology during a third of the regular class time allotted to those subjects. Early results of the program indicated that the students learned neither more nor less but that the system saved teachers considerable time. Some schools are limiting the practice to upper

classes and others are considering the establishment of the
program throughout their curricula. An extreme that could
become a reality, although it doubtless should not, was pro
posed by R. Neill McGaw, an associate professor of engineering
who won a Williams College curriculum contest with a plan
for a school at which students would have equal influence
with professors in laying out the courses of study.

While universities from Harvard to Stanford are trying to
devise more ways to put students on their own, a reverse pro
gram is being developed in other places. This is the techno
logical stimulation of mass study through television. More
than 250 colleges and universities now offer credit courses on
TV to more than 500,000 students. Airborne Educational Tele
vision is the name of one project. It is "stratovision" beamed
from a plane circling over Lafayette, Indiana, to a number of
Midwestern classrooms. The experiment, costing nearly $8,
000,000, has been dubbed "educational crop-dusting."

Automation has reached a stage where the University of
Pittsburgh obtained a $65,000 Government grant to try to
develop a computer system to schedule classes. There already
were devices to record grades, enrollment, attendance, teacher
pay, inventories and purchases. Now the university sought a
way to feed a student's record and the courses needed for a
degree into a computer and have the machine rule whether
the prerequisites had been met and whether there were con
flicts in class hours or other activity. In cases of duplication, it
was hoped that the machine would give the student an alter
nate program and then proceed to assign him to a classroom
and seat for every course. University officials reasoned that if
such a machine could be perfected, advice by robot would free
faculty advisers for more important duties.

Curriculum planning also is involving students increasingly
as are other phases of university life once reserved for faculty
and administrators. In some cases students actually participate
in planning; in others their views are sought and considered.
One of the more vocal student organizations on such matters

is the National Student Association, formed in 1947 and now representing more than 400 student bodies with more than 50 per cent of the total college and university enrollment.

The association's principal aims are to maintain academic freedom, assert student rights, improve student government and educational programs, and stimulate better international understanding and fellowship among students. It seeks to advance the student culturally, socially and physically, and wants equal rights for all. Of considerable importance is its avowed intention of encouraging students to exercise more responsibility toward their own educations.

A wave of dissatisfaction with the current offerings of higher education is sweeping the association. In a detailed statement of policy adopted at a recent convention, it made a number of recommendations, including the following:

—Colleges should encourage better preparation of high school students for advanced education and develop admission policies taking into consideration "intellectual curiosity and motivation" as well as grades.

—There should be renewed emphasis on basic, general education along with specialties because "American colleges lack devotion to the intellect, a sense of dedication and a profound respect for the education which the student should be pursuing." Solutions would include smaller classes, more independent research and closer relations between teacher and student.

—Students should be increasingly involved in both curriculum and policy planning. Curricular and extracurricular activities should be coordinated to give more meaning to the entire college experience.

The association went so far as to advocate that students should participate in establishing general admissions policies and assist in college recruiting. It is unlikely that they are about to be given that much influence, if the reactions of educators are any guide. The undergraduate of today is recognized as more mature than his predecessors but still not mature enough or possessing enough perspective and insight to supervise his own education.

College students have been found to be widening their view of the world along with their concept of the campus. After a long post-war silence, they again are speaking up on social issues—civil liberties, nuclear testing and race relations, to name a few. Interestingly, they are making themselves heard from both sides of the political fence, conservative as well as liberal.

Students from such Eastern colleges as Amherst, Smith, Mount Holyoke, Columbia and Pennsylvania shunned turkey dinners on Thanksgiving Day, 1961, to picket the White House in protest against any resumption of nuclear weapons testing. They were the spokesmen of a youth movement seeking to stir more college students into participation in the global debate on disarmament.

On the liberal side, the Student Association issued one of the early calls for help for the Congress on Racial Equality (CORE) in its sit-in protests against the segregation of chain store lunch counters in the South. By telephone and telegraph the organization mustered nation-wide campus support for the nonviolent sit-ins that eventually brought integration of many of the eating places.

A $60,000 grant from the Field Foundation was used by the association for a two-year project in the South to seek a clarification of international, national and regional aspects of human relations. Several interracial conferences were held in normally segregated communities.

Such highly publicized efforts are regarded with uncommon interest by YWCA student leaders, for, as long ago as the 1920's, "Y" college groups were holding desegregated conferences in the South and Southwest—but quietly. They began inviting Negro visitors at a time when that was a risky thing to do. In the 1930's, "Y" groups in the Southwest abandoned segregated conferences. Several women's colleges disaffiliated, amid cries of "Communism," and have not had chapters since.

In the Southern Region, extending from Virginia to Louisiana, two conferences were held each year for a time, one for white girls and the other integrated; after World War II one integrated student conference was held for all. Forty per cent of the attendance each year is made up of Negroes.

Many white girls have risked serious family dissension by attending the meetings. As a result more and more Southern colleges have dropped "Y" chapters. "The 'Y' Southern girls are extremely courageous," a national YWCA official said. "They, not the Northern girls, are pushing on racial issues. They are not those sweet little Southern girls you read about in novels."

Students have been active in public issues elsewhere. Dartmouth undergraduates picketed a New Hampshire courthouse to protest the arrest of Dr. Willard Uphaus, who refused on the ground of "Christian pacifism" to tell a state investigating committee the names of guests at his Fellowship Center. Boston students picketed an ROTC anniversary celebration by way of protesting United States military leadership and nuclear policies. Other students marched hundreds of miles to large cities to protest nuclear testing. On a more restricted level, more than 2,000 undergraduates at Bowling Green State University, in Ohio, staged a three-day demonstration to complain that they were being treated like children by the school administration. They protested a ban on good night kisses in front of girls' dormitories, "Gestapo-like" enforcement of a prohibition on beer drinking on or off campus and the so-called double jeopardy of being punished by a student traffic court after having been dealt with by a municipal judge.

The House Un-American Activities Committee stands in the middle of opposing student groups. Many organizations, ranging from the National Student Association to the Methodist Student Movement, have demanded that the committee be dissolved because of the controversial film "Operation Abolition," which was pieced together from newsreel clips of student rioting outside a committee hearing in San Francisco in 1960.

Student groups charge that the movie was assembled in such a way as to imply that all the rioters were either Communists or their "dupes."

Young conservatives idolize the House committee as well as Senator Goldwater, who has become their "knight in armor." Young Americans for Freedom, founded in 1960 by delegates from forty-four colleges and universities in twenty-four states and dedicated to fostering "the growing conservative sentiment among America's youth toward political education and action," conducted a large demonstration to support the Un-American Activities Committee. It also organized picketing of the movie *Spartacus* because of the former left-wing leanings of the scenario writer, Dalton Trumbo. The Young Americans also have demanded an investigation of the American Nazi Party as a possible "smokescreen" for Communist activity.

Out of the Young Americans for Freedom came a group of self-styled "fiery young conservatives" who organized a Freedom Party to participate in the New York City elections in 1961 as a potential training ground for campaigning for Goldwater for President in 1964.

Goldwater, meanwhile, kept busy wooing the nation's youth. He spoke to more than fifty school groups in 1960 and more than sixty-five in 1961. His audiences were made up about equally of voters and voters-to-be.

The Conservatives who support Goldwater, the liberals who attend sit-in demonstrations and the intellectuals who write theses for advanced degrees are a long way from the flasks and floozies of Dad's days in college. It is no wonder that the old grads shake their heads at the sight of the college student of today. Many an alumnus regards these young people as members of "the silent generation" because they are not rowdies, but actually they are more "modulated" than silent.

Today's college student seeks identity and recognition, but most of all he would like to be understood, as was pointed out in an appeal written by Jo Eickmann, editor of *The Daily Texan,* in an edition of the paper published for an annual

University of Texas Round-Up honoring alumni.

"Not only the buildings are different," the editorial began.

"We, too, have changed. We, the *students* . . . of the University of Texas, are not the same as when you were here.

". . . As the campus has become a massive conglomerate of glass and brick, so we have become a mass. . . . Realize that we are not dupes or rubber stamps. We will not allow ourselves to be so easily written off as that.

"Instead—ingenuous, skeptical, wise, mistaken—we are, with you, human beings—damned and redeemed; debased in our decadence and exalted in our nobility.

"We make but one human plea—*Listen to us.*

"See yourselves through us. Remember. And understand."

.6.

What's Going Wrong with Fraternities?

COLLEGE SOCIAL FRATERNITIES ARE IN TROUBLE. IT IS doubtful that they are dying, but they are seriously ill. The surest sign of their condition is that they are on the defensive, and often belligerently so, against criticism from inside and out. Racial and religious discriminaton has torn some brotherhoods and sisterhoods apart and has brought attacks from a variety of sources. Scholarship ratings in many houses have slipped, and so has the fraternity hold on campus leadership. The rate of membership growth is trailing far behind that of the academic community, causing several major societies that are weakening to merge in a search for strength.

Social fraternities—a term that encompasses sororities, too— are solidly established on many campuses, providing homes away from home for young people who have left their families for the first time. The societies contribute a partial answer to campus housing shortages and provide a kind of group living some of the more immature and socially insecure students require. Many fraternities, in an attempt to counteract their ills, have abandoned the often cruel and sometimes fatal hazings of "Hell Week" in favor of the altruism of a community "Help Week," have entered into charitable projects and have launched active scholarship-improvement programs. Fraternities that once spurned the chaperonage of housemothers now welcome the respectability of the feminine presence.

But what the organizations are doing to turn a new face to the new college world often is too little and it could be too late, despite the stentorian aid of Senator Barry Goldwater, champion of the fraternity system and hero of conservative youth, who denounces critics of the "Greek" way of life. Fraternities tend to attract the more conservative college elements and often, but not always, the wealthier or more snobbish. They listen to Goldwater when he declares that fraternities are a bastion of American democracy and joins other defenders of the fraternity system in the charge that *any* attack on the alpha and omega of college society is an assault on the Republic—in other words, downright un-American.

The crux of the fraternity problem—or at least the most deep-set symptom of illness—is the so-called policy against the inclusion of Negroes, Jews and persons of Latin origin in "white Christian" houses. Before 1950 almost every national fraternity had a "bias clause" in its constitution. Pressure from college authorities, organizations such as the Anti-defamation League of B'nai B'rith and insurgent local memberships has brought about the abolition of most discriminatory charter clauses, but in too many cases the prejudices have gone underground, so to speak, being carried into the secret rituals, which often are religious, frequently involve the use of altars and almost invariably are so steeped in Christianity that they would preclude participation by a Jew and *should* discourage any person with no religious adherence.

Some local fraternities have broken away from their national bodies in bitter disputes over pledging Negroes or Jews. Some have been ousted by the national organizations for doing so. Quite a few school administrations have ordered fraternities and sororities to abandon discriminatory practices—orders that have been obeyed. Among the more progressive institutions are Stanford, California, Michigan, Dartmouth, Williams and Amherst, to mention only a few.

Fraternities have received considerable publicity, most of it unfavorable, in their internal strife over what constitutes brotherhood. Sororities have fared better in the public eye despite the fact that their prejudices are just as deep-seated. The National Panhellenic Conference remains silent when asked about the possibility that discrimination exists in any of its twenty-nine affiliated sororites with fewer than 1,000,000 members. "Panhellenic plays its cards very close to its chest," said a prominent woman who resigned from a sorority to protest discriminatory practices. An official of Panhellenic said only that she knew nothing of any sorority problems revolving around racial or religious prejudice. As far as she and the organization were concerned, each sorority dealt with its own affairs, and that was that.

The reasons the girls have managed to keep out of the headlines except in rare instances are not easy to discover. One possible explanation is that they are not having so much difficulty because they are more conformist in their social patterns and more willing to accept the dictates of older social arbiters. Another possibility is that a girl is more likely to cry her eyes out alone than to stir up a public storm when she has been rejected by a group, no matter what the reason. A strong factor is that the very schools whose administrators and student bodies would doubtless lead and encourage attacks on sorority snobbery do not have sororities—such institutions as Vassar, Smith and Mills, for example.

Some of the leading Eastern men's colleges—most notably Williams—have pioneered the way to democratic practices in fraternity houses, amid the outraged protests of alumni. Indeed, a principal source of bias in sorority and fraternity life is found among those old grads who may have failed to mature during their four years in what some persons still call "these expensive playpens." The "alums" have a powerful influence on their organizations, and while they provide selfless service and guidance—and often financial support—to their younger brothers and sisters, there is a danger that their grip on dear old

Alpha Alpha Alpha will tighten into a stranglehold.

There is evidence in the substantial number of rebellions by local fraternities that if the racial and religious "problems" were left to young people to solve, there would be no problems. The local chapters that have broken with national fraternities on this issue have done so because the members did not want to be dictated to by old grads a thousand miles and generations away. Perhaps if national fraternities sought the counsel of their young confederates, they might find a way out of their problems and start moving forward with the rest of university life.

College administrators disagree about fraternities and sororities. The National Interfraternity Conference is inclined to rate the respective merits of colleges according to their degree of acceptance of fraternities as a "way of life." What the conference thinks of Harvard, with its clubs rather than fraternities, does not bear repeating here. But it speaks glowingly of those schools whose deans—old Greek-letter men themselves—feel that the social fraternity plays an important role in higher education by helping to produce better-rounded graduates and students who are "More Likely to Succeed."

One respected college administrator says, "The national fraternity system is dead. All that remains is to hammer in the nails on the coffin lid." Another declares just as flatly that the fraternity is the bulwark of the nation's future, and of the future of the rest of the world as well.

Statistics indicate that the bulwark is sagging, however. While fraternities are growing, they are slowing down considerably. Fraternity membership has risen only 25 per cent in the last ten years, for example, while college enrollments have shot up 50 per cent in the last five. Just as significant is the fact that the number of persons rushed by fraternities and sororities has declined, indicating that fewer are evidencing interest in being chosen. Fraternities do not want to keep pace with the staggering growth of the campus populations, of course, because they would lose too much of their exclusivity in the process. But fraternity men are becoming increasingly a nonvocal minority group, whereas they used to run most college forums and campus activities. A considerable number of pledges have been dropping out of fraternities after the freshman year because they found the competing demands of "the group" interfering with their studies. As college students become more serious and thoughtful—which has been the case since the end of World War II—they have rejected increasingly the idea of having their patterns of social behavior dictated by a century-old fraternity system.

Many local fraternities are leaving their national organizations for reasons other than issues of discrimination—a principal one being that they find their benefits from such affiliation often limited to free beds when visiting other colleges, while the national organization benefits from monthly dues.

The fraternity still is a status symbol on many campuses, particularly in the Middle West and South. Interfraternity Conference officials say that the Middle West and Southwest, most notably Goldwater's Arizona, are the real fraternity strongholds and the areas of most of the recent growth, while there has been a retreat in "decadent, socialistic" New England, a center of opposition to fraternity discrimination.

A meaningful barometer can perhaps be found in the fact that no new national sororities or fraternities of significance have been organized in recent years. Fraternities were disbanded at Norwich University, a military school in Vermont, and sororities were abolished at Randolph-Macon Woman's College in Virginia. At the same time, however, new chapters of old organizations have been formed on many campuses and old chapters have broken away from old organizations to "go local."

Fraternity people insist there really are two national fraternity systems—but it is difficult for an outsider to find out just what they mean by this, beyond the fact that the "good" fraternities seem to represent the principles of the Declaration of Independence and the Sermon on the Mount and the "bad" fraternities are publicity-seeking and socially lax.

An exchange of correspondence between the author and one of the leading authorities on fraternities sheds no light on the situation. John Robson, managing editor of *Banta's Greek Exchange,* an interfraternity magazine, and editor of the *Journal of Sigma Phi Epsilon* for twenty years, began the discussion by offering what he called the "thought-provoking" information that a Mormon fraternity recently was established in the Utah area and is thriving, while a nonsectarian fraternity established in 1948 has faded from the college scene. "It shows the paradox of spiritual homogeneity and nominal equality," Robson wrote. He added that the good fraternity system receives no publicity but grows daily while the chapters in the poor fraternity system die constantly and "their death rattle is newsworthy."

The author replied with a letter asking Robson to clarify what he meant by two fraternity systems. Are the strong fraternities in the Interfraternity Conference and the weak ones outside? the letter asked. What makes one fraternity strong and another one weak? Robson answered this way:

"Fraternity chapters by their virtuous performance or the opposite of it classify themselves into one of two systems: the good fraternity system and the poor fraternity system. Few writers on the subject of fraternity manage to achieve clarity because it is almost always the poor fraternity system that they write about. The poor fraternity system has a press; the good fraternity system does not have a press in any real sense; its glories are unsung.

"The good fraternity system is virtually eternal. Nothing happens to its chapters that is reported in the press. They go on year after year continuing to build character in young men. Many of these kept going throughout World War II and in normal times they have no difficulty whatever in attracting topnotch men.

"When writers prognosticate the death of fraternities, they reason according to the performance of the poor fraternity system which has always had its misdoings magnified in the press. Reporters find something newsworthy about the death rattle and the public learns that the fraternity is dead and concludes as a further step that it will stay dead. What happens is that the good fraternity chapters never die and the dead ones seldom stay dead—they are born again and in a considerable percentage of cases become good chapters.

"You ask: 'What makes one fraternity strong and another one weak?' The answer is easy to give but the public must think profoundly in order to understand it. It is that the good fraternity chapter follows a spiritual value system and is given the essential material with which to do this. The poor fraternity chapter follows a materialistic value system. In the case of the former the altar is real and respected. In the case of the latter it is a sham and becomes mocked."

An enclosure with the letter made it clear that Robson's thesis was based almost entirely on Christian doctrine. The material, published in the *Sigma Phi Epsilon Journal,* also described good fraternities as microcosms of good democracy and poor fraternities as microcosms of poor democracy. For example, the article said, the presence of liquor and co-eds at a fraternity's rush party means it is a club rather than a fraternity chapter.

Character building is Robson's key to fraternity success, and this, to his way of thinking, must be based on the inter-relation of God, man, the institution and the fraternity.

"In general," he observed, "our society is quite passionately occupied with the pursuit of materialistic opportunity to the subordination of spiritual values, and it follows that lax citizenship tends to produce lax fraternity chapters.

"The good fraternity chapters are true homes and the men in them maintain an atmosphere of brotherhood that is conducive of the best effort of every sort. Such a group requires close spiritual homogeneity, which is generally weakened by the introduction of groups of other races—but not in every case of course."

The device of referring to "two fraternity systems" creates

considerable semantic confusion and reflects a reluctance to get down to the facts. There is a fraternity "system," but the breakdown into "good" and "bad" would seem arbitrary, depending on individual beliefs and prejudices.

Officials of the National Student Association, which is officially neutral on the desirability of fraternities, believe that the *entire* system is declining largely because of broader student social horizons, increased use of automobiles for getting away from campus and a general easing of social taboos. Another factor almost certainly is the high marriage rate of college students. The undergraduate with a wife to go home to is less likely to belong to a social fraternity than his unmarried, oats-sowing classmate.

The comments of fraternity champions range from the almost incoherent babblings of anti-Semitic, racist old grads, who want to associate only with "white Christians," to more dispassionate discussions of the problem. It would serve no useful purpose to repeat here the more hateful things said by some spokesmen.

Goldwater's is the loudest pro-fraternity voice of all. In a widely publicized speech delivered at an Interfraternity Conference meeting, he declared that "no man can join a fraternity without being a religious man." He found that only the insidious foes of America were fighting against the fraternity system, which he said gives a boy a home, a moral atmosphere in which he is "safe," an institutional atmosphere assuring success in school and real—"not phony"—brotherhood.

His speech was reproduced in pamphlet form and reprinted in several major fraternity publications as a voice of strength, but many fraternity weaknesses are expressed in the same publications. One in particular addressed to its readers statement after statement defending fraternities and sororities; why it was necessary to present such arguments to persons who supposedly already were strong believers was not made clear.

A sorority woman wrote emotionally that the freedom of association in her organization was guaranteed in the First Amendment to the United States Constitution. She added the observation that such a guarantee meant it was all right to exclude Jews and Negroes.

Another spokeswoman for exclusivity is Mrs. Darrell Nordwall, an Alpha Chi Omega and past chairman of the National Panhellenic Conference, who was quoted in the January 1961 issue of *Banta's Greek Exchange* as saying that, contrary to what some persons might believe, sororities were not organized to solve the problems of a mixed society or serve as experimental cells for the study of sociology. They were, she maintains, designed to provide a kind of security within an association that enables a person to develop qualities of leadership, ability and responsibility that might not appear in "a less appreciative atmosphere." If this sort of association was eliminated, she says, the essence would be removed from sorority life.

Sorority women—mainly the alums—make a firm point of saying that no one *has* to join a sorority, and if a person does not like the requirements of a group from which she has been excluded, she has the constitutional right and freedom to form her own society under her own rules. What could be more fair and reasonable than that, the sorority women want to know. Fraternities are not *discriminatory*, the proponents say, but rather they are *discriminating*—in other words, they choose their members as "wisely" as they can.

Dr. George A. Bowman, president of Kent State University, has said that freedom of choice is a basic American freedom and that such a choice in fraternities is part of this freedom. Many things that are labeled discriminatory, he says, are nothing more than choice. The successful man has made the wisest choices, he adds. But he concludes that much of the discussion of discriminatory clauses has been emotional or uninformed and much that has been said on *both sides* shows confusion and a lack of thought.

Bowman argues that if discriminatory clauses involve declarations of the superiority of one man over another because of his color or racial origin, then those who subscribe to such statements are in an untenable position because science has disproved theories that there is a superior race. But, Bowman argues further, it is the right of any group to preserve its unity by defining its membership in terms of religious affiliation and racial origin—an inalienable right "as long as in so doing it does not directly or indirectly imply or declare the *superiority* of a race or religion."

One of the strongest defenders of fraternities is Dr. Willis M. Tate, president of Southern Methodist University and a member of Lambda Chi Alpha. "Sometimes," he told a National Interfraternity Conference meeting, "when fraternities are criticized, it is by those who would use the fraternity system as a whipping boy for all of their frustrations in culture or in an educational system. They try to make the fraternity system pay for the ills of the whole culture. Why they should pick out the fraternity system is not easy for me to understand."

The fraternity system *has* been picked out, however, and to its detriment. A study of the fraternity system at the University of Washington, for example, found that adverse national publicity had hurt fraternities and that membership had dropped. The negative factors found by a group of students, alumni and faculty members included discrimination, hazing, anti-intellectualism, rising costs of building and maintaining houses and overemphasis on togetherness. On the positive side, the study found mainly a growing awareness of a *need* for eliminating undesirable practices. It concluded that fraternities must offer much more than comfortable housing, and that they need more prospective members from whom to choose. It found also that fraternities tend to give status to mediocre students at the expense of those seeking academic excellence. One student was quoted as complaining about too many "Mickey Mouse" activities in the fraternity house.

The University of Illinois provides a similar picture of what has happened to fraternities. In 1960, 1,100 men were entertained during rush week and all but 100 were pledged to fraternities. In 1936 three out of ten male undergraduates at Illinois were fraternity members; in 1960 the figure was one out of eight.

The fraternity has declined—or failed to grow at its former rate—as more dormitories, many of them of Hiltonian proportions, have become available and other organizations have been formed or expanded. UCLA provides a good example of how the housing situation has changed in 20 years. In 1940 there were two women's dormitories and none for men, but there were luxurious fraternity and sorority mansions. Now there are many dormitory facilities—not enough, but enough so that students who live "on campus" need not rely entirely on fraternity facilities.

Inflationary pressures have hampered fraternities in both growing and building. It costs $150,000 to $250,000 to construct a house, and few fraternities can manage such an expense very often. Twenty years ago the average chapter operated efficiently with twenty-five to thirty boys; now the effective operating size probably is a minimum of forty-five to fifty, with a few houses having as many as 125 members.

In former times, a fraternity was most likely to expand by accepting an application for membership from a locally organized group that had decided it wanted to "go national." Now some fraternities prefer to use a missionary system, starting their own locals and guiding them "from the ground up." It costs $5,000 to $8,000 to start a chapter this way. Usually, an outstanding man is asked to transfer to a school where there is no chapter of his fraternity. He is given a scholarship, enrolls in the school and recruits enough members to form a chapter. That this has been done successfully on a number of campuses indicates there are still young people interested in joining fraternities.

There doubtless is a place—and possibly even a need—for fraternities, but they have been oversold and overrated. Nevertheless, there is no real evidence to support those who say fraternities' and sororities' days are numbered. Even with their discriminatory practices, there is no indication they will die. But they almost certainly will lose more and more of their influence if they maintain an exclusivity based on bigotry.

.7.

The Beautiful Eggheads

THE GIRL NEXT DOOR IS NOT "JUST THE GIRL NEXT DOOR" ANY more. She is Miss America.

Jimmy Jones' little sister—you know, Mary Jones, who used to wear braces on her teeth and play stickball in the street—is a choir singer, Future Teacher of America, hospital aide and high school honor student. She is one of the drum majorettes who perform acrobatics at football games on Saturday. Her calves are a bit too muscular from all the exercise, her figure is only average and it is doubtful she has ever been whistled at by a boy.

But *she* is Miss America.

In the world of the Upbeat Generation, the girl next door is the ideal. To be average is to be envied, whether on the Atlantic City boardwalk or the Sunset Strip. Once upon a time, the annual Miss America competition was a glamour contest requiring the winner to have the figure of a model, the beauty of a movie star and the ambition of a Broadway-bound actress. In Hollywood, a star lost her glitter if she stayed married too long to the same man, had babies or admitted she really was from Brooklyn, not Budapest. Now the ideal is the average, in Atlantic City and Hollywood. Miss America is the girl boys take home to meet their mothers instead of the sort they once flocked to admire at stage doors. In Hollywood, Shirley MacLaine, who looks like any boy's freckle-faced kid sister, is accorded the kind of stardom that used to be reserved for such sultry beauties as Theda Bara,

73

Greta Garbo and Hedy Lamarr.

An earlier era would have seen Miss MacLaine relegated to the role of wallflower wilting under the glow generated by such a "Middle Eastern" star as Nita Naldi—unmasked at her death as little Donna Dooley from Hoboken, New Jersey. Maria Beale Fletcher probably would not have had a chance against the bathing beauties of the 1930's who became Wampus Baby starlets, yet she became Miss America of 1962—and immediately announced plans to go to college. An organist was a recent winner of the title once sought by voluptuous Joan Blondell. Bess Myerson, the only glamour girl in the more recent Miss America crop, admits to becoming a television star without having any particular talent.

Television has become a major factor in the glorification of the average girl. The main events of the Miss America contest are televised, with the grand finale moving into living rooms across the land for most of an entire Saturday evening. When a Miss America decides she wants to have a career fling before marriage, her medium is TV. Miss Myerson found that she could be a TV celebrity—and a well-paid one—without knowing how to sing, dance or act, yet she is admired widely for her slim beauty, flashing smile, quick wit and ready answers to questions. Television has produced the no-talent star to please the audiences. People admit to their living rooms via the screen the kind of person they would allow to walk through their front doors. Miss America must be that kind of person.

The one-time beauty contests have become egghead as well as respectable. The girl who is beautiful but dumb is left to gape at the proceedings on TV and wonder what could possibly be the matter with *her*. Miss America has become a celebrity, but she goes forth clad in civic virtue instead of a bikini.

Scholarships, not screen contracts, are the only goal of most entrants in the big-money contests involving pretty girls these days. Mrs. America, of course, is rewarded with kitchen equipment for her prowess as a baking beauty, but that is only because she most likely has been to college. The unwed entrants in other contests are working their way through college on brain power. Of the thousands of scholarships available through traditional channels, most are awarded to men. Girls have welcomed the chance to enter so-called beauty competitions where the scholarship preserve is exclusively theirs; it counterbalances the athletic scholarships granted in profusion to men. As a result, the Miss America competition attracts many girls who would not otherwise dream of entering a beauty contest, not even in a Brand-Name Bra. One recent winner scored heavily because she made her own clothes. Another, who came close to winning, not only could sew but was adept at milking cows.

A total of $250,000 in scholarships is awarded to Miss America contestants from every state, Canada and a few key cities every year. The first-prize winner receives $10,000 for her education. Nearly all the others are given a total of at least $250 each, along with assorted loot. Miss America wins other prizes, among them an automobile and wardrobe and personal appearance engagements. Her total "take" runs to nearly $100,000 for her year-long tenure—enough for college and a comfortable dowry.

The metamorphosis of Miss America from a beauty queen to an "ideal average" young woman (all but one or two have married, the divorce rate is low and homemaking is the career of most) is part of the story of what is happening to youth. They want education and respectability, and they need reassurance. More important, their parents *want* them to have education and respectability, and need reassurance for *themselves* that the younger generation is going to be all right. Being Miss America has become a most respectable goal—and it is just as much a goal for mothers as it is for their daughters.

The new Miss America is accompanied to Atlantic City by her mother, where she is then handed over to an official chaperone. From the moment she is chosen until she turns her crown and scepter over to her successor, she is still more closely chaperoned and supervised. She cannot even have a date without the presence of her official "companion," who at times seems more like a WAC sergeant than an escort for the unique American concept of a queen—a girl equally at home at a campfire and a night club table.

So marked is this trend toward all-around American womanhood in contests such as the Miss America Pageant that when a resort hotel in New Jersey wanted to stage a competition to select a "Queen O'Teens," it announced: "An old-fashioned beauty contest—no talent required—limited to girls between the ages of 16 and 18." The winner was chosen on the basis of pulchritude and personality. No one inquired whether she had read any good books or if she had a formula for ending the cold war. She did not make much of an impression on the public, either, although the picture editors of tabloid newspapers were rather taken with her charms.

Today's Miss America is different. She is judged on the basis of poise, grades in school, ability to converse intelligently and talent, which covers being able to do anything from snapping pictures to hemstitching. She appears in a bathing suit briefly, and then only to satisfy the demands of newspaper editors' nostalgic for cheesecake pictures reminiscent of the good old beauty contests.

Miss Universe has taken a turn, too, possibly for the worse. A ban on bathing attire routed the contest from Long Beach, California, to be replaced by the Miss International Beauty Pageant, in which participants appear in the native attire of their countries, some of it rather voluminous and most of it prim.

Miss America Junior is selected on the basis of "the sum total of freshness, integrity, purposeful outlook, good scholarship and not much more sophistication than a 17-year-old ought to have." The 1961 Junior Miss America, Maureen Sullivan of West Haven, Connecticut, was nominated by a civic-sponsored school club on the basis of her extracurricular activities as a member of the Junior Achievement Club and French Club, cheer leader, volunteer at a Veterans Administration hospital and counselor for *Seventeen* magazine. When she was 13, Maureen decided on a career in teaching mentally retarded children; she started this training with her $5,000 contest scholarship.

When Diane Lynn Cox of Richmond, Virginia, was crowned Miss Teen-Age America late in 1961 after a week-long competition based on personality, appearance, intelligence and talent (with no bathing suit modeling allowed), she said that winning the contest would give her a chance "to help impress other teens with the necessity of good education and high, sincere ideals." Diane, the first girl to be president of the student body at George Wythe High School in Richmond and a straight A student, went on to say that her ambition was to join the diplomatic corps "to serve my country and help bring understanding and peace to the world."

The most actively egghead of the crown-seekers are the participants in the annual College Queen Contest. The twelve finalists in 1961, for example, held a total of nearly twenty-five scholarships; one girl had four. A major factor in the judging was their ability to discourse at seminars on current events, international affairs, beauty and fashion, and they were required to demonstrate their skills at safe driving. Bermuda shorts were their scantiest attire. So proper is the College Queen competition, in fact, that a Salvation Army lassie, Carole Dawn Reinhart, won the title in 1960.

The onetime beauty contests doubtless have become more intellectual because there are so many minor competitions to select "Miss Hubcap," "Miss Quick Freeze" and "Miss Etc." that it is impossible to tell one queen from another without her I.Q. rating.

The prototype of the other contests, the Miss America Pageant, features little but hard work—so much, in fact, that the mothers of also-rans have been heard to complain that if they had realized how much effort was entailed, they would not have encouraged their "little girls" to participate. No parent of a winner has ever been heard making such a statement, however.

What started in 1921 as a promotional bathing beauty parade on the Atlantic City Boardwalk now is Big Business. The selection of Miss America is a year-long process beginning with local and state contests. As many as 5,000 girls may participate from start to finish in well-organized competitions guided closely from Atlantic City headquarters with detailed instructions, includng how to tell a potential Miss America from a floozie.

"Good taste is the keynote to the success of your contest," local officials are told. "The Miss America Pageant is not a 'girlie show,' 'a bathing beauty contest,' or an amateur talent contest. It is a quest for a typical American girl, representative of the kids in your home town, or your college campus, and working in the shops of your city. The contest you are conducting will be run in such a manner that no parent or boyfriend could find any objection to its operation."

Lenora Slaughter, who has directed the pageant with such a firm yet maternal hand since 1935 that it is described by some as "Miss Slaughter's finishing school," says that Miss America— any Miss America—is "the most beautiful, gracious and talented girl" in the United States. But she adds that in her years of running the show, the *most beautiful* girl in it never has won.

"Whatever a girls wants to do in life, she can't trade on beauty alone," Miss Slaughter says. "Miss America is a girl who possesses the loveliest qualities of womanhood—grace, charm and spiritual beauty. Outward beauty is not enough. Miss America is not a bathing beauty contest. It is a pageant in which America's loveliest, most intelligent, talented, personable girls compete for the right to represent all American girlhood as an ideal girl."

In other words, what once was a "fun" contest now is about as sexy as a Sunday school picnic. Everything must have a purpose, and Miss America is included. Before Miss Slaughter took over direction of the destiny of Miss America, the winner often was a feature attraction at amusement parks, state fairs or theaters. Today it is considered inappropriate for her to participate in anything so undignified as a supermarket opening, and amusement parks are off limits.

The big-time Miss America of today bears no resemblance to the first one, a tiny, frightened blonde wearing a crown inspired by the one atop the Statue of Liberty and trembling under the folds of an American flag draped over a baggy bathing suit. She was Miss America of 1921, a 16-year-old Washington, D.C., high school girl named Margaret Gorman, who paraded on Atlantic City's Boardwalk, won her trophy, packed her overnight bag, and then went home to finish school, marry and live quietly in the nation's Capital wondering periodically whatever had possessed her to think *she* could be Miss America.

The first winner was the shortest (5 feet 1 inch), flattest-chested of all Miss Americas so far, a somewhat pear-shaped 30-25-32. She boasted no special talents, knew nothing of public speaking and never had heard of such a creature as a professional model.

Although no longer "The Atlantic City Bathing Beauty Contest," the competition still has as its principal purpose the advertisement of the resort as the place to go after Labor Day. But Miss America herself represents quite a bit more than that. She has gone through a considerable change to arrive at this stature. Physically, she is taller, older and bosomier. Mentally, she has developed to college caliber.

The girls who win the crown tend to regard their role with reverence. "I guess a girl never stops being Miss America," said Marilyn Vanderbur of Denver, Colorado, a year after she had passed the crown reluctantly to Mary Ann Mobley of Brandon, Mississippi, and had gone on to finish her studies and make commercial TV films. As for Miss Mobley, who never had a date until she was 16, she said when her time as Miss America was up: "I'm a little sad that it's over. This has been a wonderful experience. There has been a lifetime of living in one year. You go places and see things you would have no opportunity to in a normal year. But all good things must come to pass."

How do the thousands of entries become involved in this contest? Usually a girl is encouraged by her sorority, her friends, her church or her parents. In a few instances, it has been the life-long ambition of some girls—or their mothers. After applying and being accepted for the preliminaries, a girl appears first in her local contest, in which she goes through judging rounds patterned after those of the Atlantic City finals. After collecting prizes on the local level, she goes to the state contest, where the finalist to go to Atlantic City is chosen, with judging still along the same lines.

Some of the girls then go through an intense grooming period. Susan Diane Bronson, then 19, of San Lorenzo, California, for example, was the most manicured, primped, preened and trained of the record stable of entries in 1959. She spent weeks in Hollywood learning to apply eye shadow and acquiring a talent (dancing), and took lessons in poise and public speaking. Other girls went to modeling and charm schools to "train" for the pageant. A few went on diets. West Virginia's Janet Marie Hill studied dramatics for the 1959 contest. Esther Olney, Miss Delaware of 1960, made at least 150 personal appearances in her home state before going to the finals. Miss North Carolina of any year is the Governor's official hostess and can count on making more than $20,000 in public appearances, before and after the finals, no matter what the judges in Atlantic City think of her.

The local and state competitions are sponsored not by theaters or amusement parks, as in the old days, but by Junior Chambers of Commerce in most instances, and also by newspapers, a modeling school and at least one church.

So successful has the pageant become, with commercial sponsors investing enormous sums in the enterprise and nation-wide interest in the outcome, that other major contests for girls have been patterned after it to some degree. Perhaps the other competitions have not copied the Miss America show exactly, but they have taken on the same dignified mien, giving girls a status they never have had before by letting them prove that they are able to do more than the Pachanga or the Twist. The new positive approach to pulchritude is more in the interest of young people than adult audiences. It singles out the normally attractive girl, rather than the three-dimensional freak. And it gives many teenage girls a goal—for a college education, for travel or perhaps just for recognition as an individual.

Many persons still regard contests such as those for Miss America, the College Queen, Mrs. America and the rest as just so much fluff, even without the bathing suits, scarlet robes trimmed with cotton "ermine" and tin tiaras. There are, to be sure, some theatrical aspects about the contests but these decrease every year. Those who take the proceedings seriously—and many justifiably do—feel that America has a queen at last in the "girl next door."

.8.

The Teen-Age Girl:
Malnourished American

THE FUTURE MOTHER OF AMERICA IS THE MOST POORLY FED member of her family. By eating improperly in her teens, she is endangering her own health and that of her children. Her day often begins with little or no breakfast and frequently is filled with snacks of "empty calories" that add pimples and pounds but provide little nourishment. "Hidden hunger"—in a land of plenty—may go undetected by a mother so busy working, assisting the League of Women Voters or following the latest fad diet that she has little time to plan and prepare well-balanced meals for her children.

A teen-age boy is likely to be somewhat better off for no reason except that he eats more than his sister and is bound to consume more nutrients in the process. His diet is far from ideal, for in his teens he may be overeating his way to a heart attack in his forties. But what he consumes is better for him now than his sister's intake is for her, particularly in view of the fact that she may bear her first child before she is 20, as 25 per cent of all mothers do.

The inadequate regimen of brother and sister need not be attributed to a lack of funds. Indeed, even in impoverished American families there are few cases of rickets today. Some of the most poorly nourished youngsters—and that covers the overfed as well as underfed—come from well-to-do families that seem to have little awareness of the need for proper nutrition. It is in these homes that meals are so disorganized that youngsters are left to forage for their own breakfast or lunch and sometimes dinner—and what they select from the well-stocked refrigerator seldom is what the doctor would order.

Malnourished teen-agers persist despite—and in some cases, perhaps, because of—the growth of a new science known as food technology, which has seen its greatest advance since the outbreak of World War II. This specialty has attracted nutritionists, dieticians, home economists, sociologists and publicists, all intent on improving or changing the eating habits of the nation, principally its younger members. Some of these experts are motivated solely by an interest in the welfare of the individual, the nation or mankind. Others, at least in part, work for the welfare of the food industry or some element of it, with the result that the teen-age consumer and just about everyone else is bombarded from all sides with appeals to eat more sugar, pork sausage, bread, cereal, butter, margarine or eggs or, alternatively, *not* to eat one thing or another. The teen-ager is confronted with calorie charts, recommended serving sizes of dishes and all manner of conflicting appeals and information, so that he tends to keep on doing what he was doing all along—namely, eating improperly.

Nutritionists generally agree that older teen-agers, because they are put more on their own, have worse eating habits than younger ones. They develop dietary shortcomings that leave them without adequate vitamin C, or ascorbic acid, which is in citrus fruits, berries, greens, cabbage and peppers. They are deficient, too, in vitamin A, which is found in yellow vegetables and fish; thiamine, which is in beans, fruits, cereal grain, pork, liver and spinach, and riboflavin, which is in liver, poultry, milk, fish and cottage cheese, and which, according to the small print on boxes, is abundant in cereal, cake mixes, flour and many other food items. Shortages of iron, especially necessary during the menstrual period, are found in the diet of many a teen-age girl because of her low intake of liver, dark green leafy vegetables, chicken and eggs. Too often a girl will substitute potato chips or a candy bar chock full of calories for something more nutritious.

The Bill of Particulars against the teen-ager is a long one. Here is some of the evidence:

- The National Research Council found that six out of ten girls and four out of ten boys had inadequate diets.

- A study of nearly 7,400 Chicago children showed 72 per cent with unsatisfactory diets regardless of family income.

- Cornell University researchers found that 50 per cent of a large group of New York State teen-agers were malnourished.

- A Nebraska study concluded that the worst dietary offenders were girls between 13 and 15.

- Meals eaten by 180 Iowa teen-agers during a week showed deficiencies in calcium, iron and vitamin C.

- Sixty-five per cent of the children in 6,000 families studied by the Pennsylvania Department of Health were deficient in at least one essential nutrient.

- Several studies indicate that at least 19 per cent of all children are underweight and at least 22 per cent are overweight. Both conditions were found most often among girls, mainly older ones. Compulsive eating and irregular meals were the principal offenders.

- Older teen-agers studied showed tendencies to gain weight during the first months away from home, either in a job or at college. This leads many college women to engage in potentially harmful reducing procedures or to return to the irresponsible eating habits of their high school days.

A teen-age girl should consume between 2,400 and 2,600 calories a day, as compared with 3,100 to 3,600 for a boy, according to the recommended daily dietary allowances compiled by the National Research Council. The fewer calories a girl eats, the more she must make every bite count. But the teen-age girl fears she will get fat if she eats eggs and drinks milk at breakfast. She wants to be popular, so she eats what her friends do. Milk is a baby drink as far as she is concerned. You simply do not sip it to be sociable on dates unless gobs of rich ice cream and plenty of flavoring are mixed with it.

Young people, including college students, accept food fallacies as fact. It is difficult to convince a girl munching "de-starched" potato chips that the fat in them contains more calories than the eliminated starch did. Another widely believed fallacy is that popcorn is a good substitute for meat and milk; actually popcorn is mainly calories. Skipping meals is a highly regarded weight reduction system in the teen-age world. That practice sometimes results in a weight increase instead, for the girl who does not eat lunch is likely to stuff herself at dinner.

The damage done by poor eating habits in the teens can be carried into the rest of a person's life, with more frequent visits to the dentist and doctor and possible birth defects in children. Fifty-three per cent of all girls between 15 and 19 either are married or have been. Those who are malnourished often are poor obstetrical risks, and their babies may be premature or sickly. Six per cent of the deaths among girls 18 and 19 are due to complications of pregnancy and childbirth.

Who is to blame for malnourishment among youngsters? Parents come in for the greatest amount of criticism. By the time their teen-age daughters get married and become pregnant, it is too late to correct childhood nutritional deficiencies. Proper eating habits must be followed in all the years before pregnancy, and who but the parents are basically responsible for overseeing this?

The American Dietetic Association says parents have failed to encourage their children in good eating habits. Mothers are the real culprits, dieticians say, because they have so many commitments outside the home that they leave children to run their own lives. Furthermore, parents often set poor examples. Dr. Fredrick J. Stare, a Harvard nutritionist, says that on a percentage basis there are just as many problem eaters among parents as among teen-agers. Cornell experts found that only 25 per cent of the housewives they polled in Rochester and Syracuse, New

York, had even a "fair understanding" of the nutritional demands of their families.

Mothers come under the fire of nutritionists also for thinking a plump, overfed baby is a healthy, happy baby. The overstuffing of children in infancy establishes food patterns they may never overcome. Mothers err also in serving fancy, high-calorie dishes to children when they should be providing simpler, more nutritious fare. Some mothers persist in serving unbalanced meals and in leaving milk in the sun (where it loses part of its vitamin content), throwing out vitamin-rich outer leaves of lettuce or boiling the vitamin C out of cabbage.

The mothers of today's mothers were even less nutrition-conscious. The word vitamin did not come into the homemaker's vocabulary until some time in the 1920's, when spinach was the center of dietary attention. Later, when vitamins were synthesized into pills, the spinach inundation subsided.

New foods have kept coming along, not necessarily nutritionally ideal products but different and tasty ones. More fortified foods are sold—enriched breads and flours and milk with vitamin D and juices with vitamin C. There is a constantly changing and expanding variety of mixes and frozen foods, even including pizza pie. New food products are added to grocery shelves at a rate of about 200 a month; an estimated 80 per cent of all the items now on sale were unavailable in their present form before World War II. Americans unquestionably are the *most* fed people in the world. It is their own fault if they are not the *best* fed.

Nutritionists and home economists have gained new stature in the food revolution. When home economics was introduced in land-grant colleges in Iowa, Kansas and Illinois in the 1870's, it was for the purpose of teaching cooking and sewing. Now elaborate courses are offered in hundreds of institutions, with homemaking only one of many subjects. Among the others are training for professional work in teaching, agricultural extension services, dietetics, institutional administration and journalism. The range is so broad in both high school and college that education for "consumership," family living and management of home finances is offered. Some courses also include child development and decision-making as academic subjects.

World War II stimulated interest in home economics and nutrition. Many men were better fed than ever after they entered the armed forces. At home, their families cultivated victory gardens and consumed large quantities of vegetables and fruits during the period of meat rationing. War plants provided free lunches to workers to make sure they ate at least one proper meal a day—a practice that has been continued in peacetime by a number of companies.

A major development in food technology came at the outset of the war with the formation of the Nutrition Foundation to work on food projects. The foundation soon branched into basic research that stimulated the development of a hard core of professional nutritionists. Fifty companies involved in the food industry now finance the work of the foundation, which seems to emphasize nutritional uses for cereal grains.

The Department of Agriculture reports that some of the wartime progress vanished with peace. When it was possible to return to former bad habits, many persons lost no time in doing so. Despite expanded nutritional education campaigns, the Department reported, the basic American diet has remained largely unchanged in the last decade. When the economy is strong, consumption of starches drops, while that of dairy products, meat, fish, poultry and other prestige foods rises—except among the teen-agers, who live in a dietary world of their own.

Young athletes live still more removed from the rest of society, nutritionally speaking. The training table, contrary to popular belief, is a potential mischief-maker. Dr. Robert S. Goodhart, a leading nutritionist and research director of the National Vitamin Foundation, has concluded that the young athlete is in dire need of being reached by nutrition education. With the encouragement of coaches, athletes eat large quantities of meat to give them strength. This puts a heavy burden on the body; the bigger and stronger you become, the greater the burden. That is all right, as long as a boy is letting off great amounts of energy on the football field, track or tennis court. But if, when he goes into a job, he continues to eat as much as he did when he played football or baseball, he will put on weight, and this can be the road to a coronary heart attack.

There are many other food groups, each with its own nutritional theories. The National Youthpower Project of the National Food Conference professes to speak for sixty food industry organizations in campaigning for nationwide community drives to encourage young people to eat more of the "right" foods and less of the "wrong" ones. Sugar Information, Incorporated, plugs away at trying to convince consumers that sugar builds extra energy for work and play and that while artificial sweeteners add taste, sugar provides fuel and flavor.

Much of such nutrition education, however valuable it may be, is economically motivated and sometimes contradictory. When the dairy industry has a surplus, it persuades a governor to promote the high consumption of milk and eggs. The National Livestock and Meat Board, in a chart for teen-agers, recommends pork sausage for breakfast for a 16-to-19-year-old girl. Cereal and bread are emphasized on a "balanced diet" menu circulated by the Nutrition Foundation. The National Dairy Council endorses ice cream as a healthful snack. What happens to the teen-ager's diet depends on whose chart he reads.

Nevertheless, in the midst of the conflicts that are bound to result from the declarations of the nutrition "experts," the teen-ager is at last getting help. A major hope for his future is the rise of a new area of medical specialization: treatment by doctors specially trained for teen-agers as pediatricians are for small children and geriatricians for old people. The teen-age specialist is called an ephebiatrician or hebiatrician, both labels based on ancient Greek words for young men and women. The doctor keeps charts of the growth and development of his young patients and, during periodic examinations, talks with them about their health and emotional problems.

Schools are another channel for nutritional information. The

Federal school lunch program has provided 20,000,000,000 healthful lunches. Classroom discussions of food also have become an important nutritional aid, on the theory that children are more likely to heed the advice of almost any adult except their parents. Why this should be presents a tantalizing question, but the situation exists just as surely in the realm of the facts of eating as in the "facts of life."

Many things can and are being done for and by youngsters to encourage them to eat properly. Here are some of the guidelines that adults can provide:

—The key to successful nutrition education is to convince young people that they must eat properly in order to look and act their best and to be popular. Schools, foundations and other groups should provide literature emphasizing the role of food in building vigor, good looks, a good figure or physique and a pleasing personality. Youngsters respond to appeals to eat properly for what it will do for them socially and on the athletic field.

—Any nutritional program should be planned on a long-range basis, not as a one-shot lecture or discussion. Instruction should penetrate every classroom and young people's club. Essays on food can be written in English classes. History courses can go into the development of farming and food-processing techniques. Science courses can include discussions of vitamins and other nutrients. The mathematics of farming and home budgeting fits logically into a class in arithmetic.

—The reasons for poor dietary habits often are hidden. It is up to teachers and other adults to try to find these reasons, always being careful not to take sides in a touchy parent-child relationship. One way to do this is to assign each pupil to do all of the family food shopping and menu planning for a week; to keep a record of everything eaten, at home and away from home, by every member of the family for two weeks; to keep a list of food eaten between meals for a week and total the calories, and to keep a food diary for a month with analyses of the contents and calories of each meal. Pupils also might survey community food habits in interviews with neighborhood families and classmates and study the dietary practices of teen-agers and recommend improvements.

—Every family should sit down to at least one meal a day together, and preferably two. It is almost impossible to coordinate an entire family's program for lunch together, but a breakfast prepared by the wife and mother and a family dinner at night are both possible and desirable. Children eat better meals under the gaze of adults than they do when they serve themselves. Often, when left to prepare their own meals, they would rather go hungry than bother.

—Coordinated nutritional activities should be organized by schools and medical, dental and public health groups, which then could involve parents through clubs and food markets, where nutrition information should be made available.

Specific programs have been started in a number of places, all of them too new to warrant any conclusions. Children in the elementary school at Sparta, New Jersey, are learning about nutrition in classes in English, art, science, health and social studies. They began their long-range program by listing their food intake for two weeks. A compilation showed that only 26 per cent had eaten adequate breakfasts, 41 per cent were low in vitamin C consumption and 45 per cent had spurned their morning milk.

Different grade levels received assignments based on their learning abilities. First-graders visited a dairy and wrote sentences about nutrition such as, "We need fruit to keep us healthy." Older children learned in social-studies classes where food came from and how it was processed. A "two-bite" club was organized to persuade children to try new foods. Games were played involving covering the eyes and trying to identify foods by taste or smell. It was not unusual for a child to be unable to name a vegetable he always had refused to touch when he saw it on his plate at home.

A weight-reduction camp is conducted for obese teen-age girls on Cape Cod. Every camper is required to engage in active sports—something fat girls frequently spurn. They are served low-calorie foods and fruit snacks, and careful records are kept of their progress. The secret of whatever success is achieved is the changing of eating habits—which is difficult for a girl to do after going on a "crash diet" or pruning off pounds with liquid "meals." There is one sure way to lose weight and keep it lost and that is to find out where you went wrong and make permanent corrections, even if it means you never will eat ice cream or peanut-butter sandwiches again.

This weight-reducing camp is an oasis for the overfed teenage girl. There are not many places like it. The problem eater is left largely to the whims of the food faddists, whose diets have ranged from skimmed milk and bananas three times a day to an enormous repast once a day and nothing else. Leaders in the nutrition field are convinced that if they were left to carry out their long-range programs, they might achieve some measurable results by the time today's teen-ager is on the brink of grandmotherhood. Meanwhile, they worry about new discoveries that change nutritional concepts. The foods they are "selling" today may turn out to be less desirable than items they are ignoring.

Take the case of spinach. It was *the* vegetable in the 1920's and 1930's. Countless children who detested it were force-fed spinach by mothers who had been led to believe that this was the only way to prevent malnutrition. Spinach was "good for you" because it contained more vitamin A than almost any other food and yet was low in calories. It was inexpensive, too. Nutrition pioneers extolled its virtues, as a result of which many a parent of today cannot swallow a forkful of the vegetable, let alone serve it to his children.

And now there has been added a sort of "whispering campaign" against spinach, possibly fomented by a nutritionist for whom the enforced consumption of the vegetable was a traumatic experience in childhood. The new word on spinach is that it contains a large amount of oxalic acid, which prevents the absorption of calcium when milk and spinach are consumed at the same meal.

All of which should provide the food world with a moral, as expressed by that little girl who, in *The New Yorker* cartoon of a generation ago, spoke volumes in condemnation of the faddists in an exchange with her spinach-promoting mother. It went like this:

"But it's broccoli, dear."

"I say it's spinach, and I say 'the hell with it!' "

.9.

The Young Spenders

"Get 'em young!" is the rallying cry of American business and industry in their bid for the youth market.

From the tots, who sit for hours staring back at the cycloptic boob tubes in their living rooms, to teen-agers, who carry blaring transistor radios wherever they go and invest heavily in "pop" records, movie tickets, cosmetics and gasoline, the younger generation is the darling of Madison Avenue, Detroit and Hollywood. The commercial courtship of the juvenile consumer from the time he awakens until he goes to bed at night is aimed at what he will spend both tomorrow and when he grows up.

The teen-age contribution to this youth jackpot is estimated conservatively at $10,000,000,000 a year in direct spending, plus billions more in family spending influenced—or wangled—by youngsters. No one has produced more than an educated guess on how many dollars are sent into the capitalistic whirl by small children who memorize TV commercials before they learn to recite Mother Goose and identify products by their televised trademarks without knowing how to read a word. But it is known—all too well, in some households—that when an announcer exhorts a child to send his mother right down to the corner grocery for X's crunchy cereal, Y's quintuple-enriched starchless bread, or Z's nutritious, vitamin-packed candy bars, the little tyke cannot wait to oblige. Junior declares in *that* voice that he will not eat a single flake of another brand of cereal because it does not come with a prize in every package, and besides, the man on television said that Crunchies were the only cereal that would enable a boy to grow into a man. Junior—and his sister, too, of course—sets up another howl when confronted with a cookie that has not been endorsed by his favorite canine TV star or was not mentioned by Captain Kangaroo. His frantic mother, willing to do anything—short of smashing the television set—finally concedes that she really is hooked when Junior sings the same nerve-jarring commercial over and over in his slightly off-key and—at this moment—irritatingly piping voice. Everyone commented "how precocious" when he learned to lisp commercials without any parental coaching, but now his mother wishes that his first word had been "Daddy," rather than the name of a deordorant advertised on TV.

Small children graduate from being an impecunious—but highly effective—pressure group to a powerful combination of direct spender and influence when they reach their teens—which in this case actually begin at the age of about ten—and either receive allowances, get part-time jobs or derive their purchasing power from both sources. The disposable income of the 25,000,000 teen-agers is estimated at an average of just under ten dollars a week for each girl and just over that sum for each boy—and an army of companies is after this wealth.

In times past, when youngsters had negligible incomes and their parents did the bulk of their buying for them, the most they ever purchased were wax whistles filled with a sweet colored liquid, penny licorice sticks or school supplies. The principal advertisements aimed at children were hand-painted signs in stationery store windows announcing that new stocks of pencils and pens were available for the start of the school year. World War II contributed largely to changing that picture, just as it changed just about everything else. Teen-age independence was born when parents were absent—fathers at war and mothers at war work. After the war, mothers continued to work. One out of five families moves every year. Fathers travel more in their business. Mothers find increasing reasons to be away from home.

All these factors—and, obviously, many others—have put teen-agers more on their own and, at the same time, made them more reliant on one another. They influence each other's lives in many ways, one of them being consumer habits. Children, like adults, follow the herd instinct in buying, and because they are somewhat segregated from much of the rest of society, teen-agers, particularly girls, tend to set clothing styles that have little to do with Paris or New York and yet are almost uniformly the same across the country. When mothers hurriedly shortened skirts a few years ago to follow the dictates of Christian Dior, for example, their teen-age daughters kept their skirts long, their sweaters baggy and their heavy bobby socks pulled as high as they would go.

Youngsters are more willing to try new products than are their parents, however, and that is one major reason why much advertising is aimed at them. They were among the first consumers to accept frozen TV dinners and filter cigarettes. Many youngsters contribute heavily to the final decision on what make or model car the family should buy or the brand of the next television set. Girls influence mothers in the choice of living room furniture and kitchen equipment.

In their wooing of the consumers of tomorrow—"developing consumers," they are called in the advertising trade—advertisers are using all their motivationally researched wiles to indoctrinate young spenders. Business and industry never rest; they start with before-school radio and television commercials and end at night with eloquently shouted—announcers never *talk*—plugs that children can take to bed and dream upon. Young people's magazines contain advertisements promoting all manner of things of obvious interest to teen-agers. An insurance company, in the belief that you cannot get to them young enough, produced an institutional ad urging a young man not yet arrived at puberty to put aside his baseball bat and think for a moment about his retirement half a century hence.

At school, children are beset with a variety of educational materials provided by business concerns, ostensibly in an altruistic manner but admittedly to attract future customers. American business is said to spend more money on its high school teaching-aid programs than all the schools combined invest in textbooks. A peanut butter company, for example, has distributed the history of the peanut. A paper manufacturer has published a little volume describing how trees are converted to paper. Personal cleanliness is emphasized in a pamphlet by a maker of toilet preparations. A pattern company provides domestic science teachers with helpful materials for sewing classes. Charts and graphs on proper eating—including the products of the companies involved—are distributed in large numbers by food processors.

Sometimes teachers manage to pique the "public-spirited" industries by carefully snipping the commercials from donated materials, but in many cases the ads are slipped in so cleverly that it is difficult to excise them. This is particularly true of so-called educational movies offered in almost endless supply, free, by hundreds of companies. It is equally difficult to decommercialize a visit to a factory or a dairy.

An example of the effectiveness of efforts to make youngsters brand-conscious—and conscious of *one* particuar brand—is provided by the General Electric Company, giant of the appliance industry and intent on remaining so. Scholastic magazines conducted a survey early in 1961 on "socio-economic attitudes of high school youth," in which GE ranked at the top of lists of companies students would choose to work for, of companies leading in scientific research and of companies doing the most outstanding jobs in atomic energy, missiles, rockets and engineering. This meant that GE had succeeded in selling its corporate image to its captive audience of high school boys and girls through provision of scientific educational aids accompanied by reminders of their source.

General Motors was mentioned second in order of frequency by the students, probably because of its extensive scholarship programs and teaching aids but also undoubtedly because of the magazine it publishes and sends free to every newly licensed young motorist in the country. The publication reached more than 1,500,000 teen-agers in 1961.

The generosity of the industries that spend large amounts of money on education of the young is commendable, but the inclusion of subtle consumer education techniques may be open to criticism. Adults won a battle not long ago against having to listen to radio commercials on commuter trains in New York on the ground that they would be a captive audience. These same adults send their children to schools in which taxpayers are providing a medium for advertisers to reach a potentially lucrative market. It might cost the commercial interests far more money to spread their messages through other channels, paying for time or space and, in the case of broadcasting, providing a stipend for the announcer, who in the schoolroom is supplanted by an often inadequately paid teacher, in many instances unaware that she is allowing herself to be used for and by commercial interests.

Another "free ride" for the advertiser is found in the toy store, where the consumer pays the bill. Parents actually buy baking sets containing miniature packages bearing the labels of products available in markets. A popular modernistic style of dishes is available in plastic miniatures, with the name of the designer on them. Makers of medical supplies collect royalties from the sale of toy kits containing samples or "reasonable facsimiles" of their products—the sort of thing that was obtainable free a generation ago by anyone sending in a coupon clipped from a magazine advertisement. Children who used to collect samples of tooth paste, soap and other merchandise for the price of a postage stamp now get the same kind of items through toy stores. The public is buying what the manufacturers used to give away, and in doing so is helping to indoctrinate children in the uses of brand-name products.

Youth is courted on other levels of commercialism as well. Older teen-agers are lectured from one side on the potential dangers of cigarettes as possible causes of cancer or heart disease and are showered from the other with free samples of cigarettes passed out on college campuses in efforts to persuade them to begin smoking or to switch brands. When a new, nontobacco cigarette was introduced, the manufacturer frankly hoped to do most of his business with a new generation of smokers who would not recognize the sharp difference between his somewhat pungent brand and cigarettes packed with real tobacco. The cigarettes, at last report, still were in the process of being perfected.

Contests are a favorite device among companies trying to share the youth market. A pencil manufacturer awarded generous cash prizes to the youngsters who drew the most skillful pencil sketches. For completion of a jingle, a cheese company rewarded the first-place winner with a free telephone of his own for a year. A gold-plated typewriter went to the top-ranking writer of an essay on Thanksgiving in a contest sponsored by a typewriter company. A giant of the food industry conducts an annual search for the homemaker of tomorrow.

Trademarks and packaging also are important lures. Mickey Mouse has sold all manner of products, from cereal to watches. Davy Crockett, in his TV days of glory, had children eating from dishes bearing his likeness and going to bed in coonskin hats. Elvis Presley and Hopalong Cassidy have shown a similar interest in establishing product links.

Cooking editors of newspapers have been known to write columns fostering commercial forays into the youth market, as was the case with a series of recipes involving cereal, one of them calling for Crunchies topped with ice cream—for breakfast. A major shoe company seeks the custom of the young by offering to immortalize the shoes of athletic stars by coating them in bronze the way "baby's first shoes" are preserved. Imagine using a pair of gunboat-size, cleated football shoes as bookends for Keats, Shakespeare and the Bible!

Expeditions in search of the dollars of the young are not made without careful research. The teen-age market is thoroughly and constantly scrutinized because it is ever-changing. Youngsters are even more avid brand-switchers than their parents and they are always looking for something new.

Various studies have shown that four out of five girls cook or bake at home and that they spend an average of more than an hour a day on the telephone and a "median period" of two hours and thirteen minutes a day listening to the radio. They are more likely to own popular records than classical. They spend $300,000,000 a year on cosmetics. Boys average forty-two minutes a day on the telephone and two hours in radio listening. They invest an average of $163 a year in clothes, just a little more than half of what girls spend. The biggest drain on the boys' finances is food, with sports and dates ranking next. A total of more than $200,000,000 in teen-agers' dollars goes for their own automobiles and gasoline, to which must be added an almost inestimable amount being spent by parents who allow their youngsters to use family cars.

Teen-agers have been found to constitute the smallest television audience. They stray away from the screen to read books or listen to hi-fi, possibly because they were satiated with TV when younger. Eventually they wander back to the set as young adults. In the meantime they discover the movies, which are within the financial reach of boys taking girls out on their first dates. Teen-agers have been credited by Hollywood leaders with saving the movie industry. Some estimates indicate that the teen-aged 11 per cent of the population makes up at least half of all movie audiences.

The record industry also bows to teen-agers for keeping the turntables of many music companies spinning overtime. One company reported that 90 per cent of its single records and half of its albums were bought by youngsters.

The approach to teen-agers, whether commercially inspired or not, always is sociological. Terms such as "peer groups" and "teen subculture" invariably crop up in discussions of the facts that teen-agers like to be with other teen-agers and that they live in a world of their own. It took a survey to inform advertising men that teen-agers are vitally interested in the opposite sex, in being popular, in having pleasing appearances and in being healthy. Advertisers who were given the benefit of this expertise were advised not to preach or talk down to teen-agers and never, never to use so-called teen-age jargon, because young people seldom talk the way advertising copywriters think they do. High-priced experts further advised advertisers to be "completely honest" in presenting a product to young people, who are quick to spot a phony and might spurn the products of a company that had misled them.

There is cause for worry about all this encouragement of acquisitiveness of young people, and many youths begin to question it themselves as they emerge from their teens. One of the darkest spots lies in the area of thrift, which seldom is mentioned in appeals for the dollars of the children of prosperity.

Young people are encouraged to invest in securities, and the New York Stock Exchange seldom misses an opportunity to publicize budding tycoons. The amount invested is negligible, however, for saving is not one of the uphearted activities of the young. Bankers are concerned about the vast spending by this segment of the population and report that savings are relatively low as compared with the sums of money that flow into—and out of—teen-age hands. The American Bankers Association said that $234,620,000 was on deposit in 6,341,000 school savings accounts in 1960. This was described as a record, and much more money was in regular accounts in children's names. However, an association survey disclosed that slightly more than half of all teen-agers do not save money—at home or in banks. Girls were found to be more thrifty than boys, but not much; the percentages were 51.1 for girls and 46.2 for boys. The savings that are accumulated shrink as youngsters grow older and find more things to buy. Most of those with no savings said they did not have anything left after paying their expenses. Some said that inflation would make any savings worth very little anyway; others that there was nothing to save for. Quite a few reflected their parents' buying habits in making the observation that there was no reason to save as long as one could obtain almost anything he wanted on the installment plan.

The buy-now-pay-later philosophy of the adult world is entering the teen-age culture, too, in the form of the credit card and charge account. Some stores that have adopted credit plans for youth regard them as a constructive way to teach children how to spend. There also is the possibility that the youngster who buys now will keep on shopping in the same store later.

A teen-ager's eligibility for a charge account varies according to the store. Some merchants honor the credit of youngsters whose parents are established customers. Others make accounts available to children as young as 12 years old if their parents approve. Teen-agers usually are allowed to open their own accounts. Although in many instances minors are not legally liable for debts, merchants have found that junior charge-account holders generally are better risks than adults.

Young people, abetted and encouraged by those who wax rich on their spending power, often seem to be in the clutches of conspicuous consumption, perhaps even conspicuous waste. Their individual purchasing power rises constantly and so does the number of teen-agers, indicating that the youth market of the future is bound to be vast.

Business presumably will step up its efforts to claim most of their money. With the costs of college education rising to a danger point and threatening to go higher, commercially inspired donors might consider diverting some of their youth market profits to more and larger scholarships and devoting less money to classroom commercials.

The advertisers might defend themselves against critics who question the morality of draining the juvenile purse by conducting advertising campaigns saying, in effect, "We want you to be our customers some day, but not now. Put your money in the bank for a college education and we will welcome you as consumers when you are grown up."

That sort of advertisement is not very likely to turn up soon, thus leaving the school as the major front for combating the commercial exploitation of children. First, the schools should screen every contribution from commercial donors of materials and make certain the contents are entirely educational. Offerings that do not pass this scrutiny should be rejected. Then, the schools should introduce thorough courses in consumer education, including thrift, in which young people are let in on selling techniques and taught how to judge products. Something needs to be done—and soon—to curb the commercialization of the classroom.

.10.

The Junior Joiners

A GIRL WE SHALL CALL SUSAN IS A CAREER TEEN-AGER. SHE has been a very busy girl, winning scholastic honors throughout high school and engaging in so many other activities that even her family sometimes has wondered where she found the time and energy for it all. Susan began her career of busyness in high school, where she became a member of the Latin, Spanish and Ski Clubs, the Cubs and the Thespians, as well as president of the Junior Class, secretary of the Student Council, treasurer of the Girls Athletic Association, the "best all-round senior girl" and "Zonta Girl of the Month"—and still managed to graduate with a National Merit Letter of Commendation for her good grades.

This is only part of the picture of a teen-ager at work, however. Susan was just as busy off the school grounds as on, belonging to the local Association of Teen-Agers, the Young Republicans, the United Christian Youth Movement, Methodist Youth Fellowship and Junior Achievement, which named her a "queen." Her affiliations were wide-ranging. She was a Worthy Adviser of the Do-Good Girls, taught swimming for the local Recreation Department, worked on muscular dystrophy and cancer drives, helped prepare Easter Seal appeals, and sold poppies, forget-me-nots and carnations on the days set aside for street corner fund-raising efforts.

All these activities did not make Susan an odd-ball among

103

her fellow teen-agers. She probably would have been considered more "out" than "in" if she had not been so busy. Susan typifies the Junior Joiner, who often makes organization men and women seem anti-social by comparison. In their search for recognition, identity and careers, youngsters have become enthusiastic joiners—and there are more groups to be joined than ever before. A parent who belongs to a few clubs—or none— may have a son or daughter with active membership in ten. The teen-ager joins clubs that are sponsored by the organizations his parents belong to or that encourage career specialties, outdoor lore, sports, hobbies, civic betterment or religious uplift. His gregariousness takes him where his friends go, and they go where he does, and all of the youngsters are plunged into a teen-age status race in which they compete against adults, each other and even themselves, with every waking hour being consumed by classes, homework, extracurricular activities and the earning of money to finance the high cost of adolescence.

The young American thus is confronted early in life with situations in which he must make choices. Often, obviously, youngsters avoid making choices by joining every organizaton that invites their membership. Many persons, young or old, are more stimulated when they have what appears to be too much to do than when they have so-called spare time; they operate at the top of their form when challenged by a variety of interests. But others doubtless would fare better if they were to concentrate on a few activities in which they *really* were interested. The adults who encourage youngsters to become joiners often are motivated by a desire to "keep the kids off the streets," reduce the juvenile delinquency rate or fight the Communist menace than by a wish to develop the individual. Perhaps those who counsel young people should encourage them to learn to make choices now—even to *force* themselves to make choices— so that when they are faced with making their first decisions as adults, the process may be a relatively painless one.

Just how much of a choice there is for teen-agers can be seen in a rough tabulation of the statistics on a score of the

herishing what remains of its old suffragette fire and its
ealous protection of the working girl, remains a feminist move-
nent in the sense that its leaders feel there should be an organi-
ation with a program tailored to suit the needs of women.

Apartness is just as important as togetherness, "Y" leaders
eel. In fact, togetherness has been so overemphasized and mis-
ised that it has come to be regarded as far from the sociological
deal—in YWCA circles, at any rate. A few years ago togetherness
vas offered as a solution for all manner of problems, mainly
uvenile delinquency. But family programs and togetherness
aave come under fire with a new awareness that no individual
:an survive if he has to put his faith entirely in a group; he
1eeds to develop his own resources and be able to get along
ay himself when the group is not available.

That is the new philosophy of YWCA activities. The "Y"
:ncourages the togetherness of girls of the same age or interests,
of boys and girls of the same age (sociologists call these "peer
groups") and of parents and children. But it also deals with
vomen and girls as individuals, encouraging each to achieve
aer full potential in society and trying to save each from being
:rushed by the group.

A feminist refrain runs through the "Y" program. The
organization may, indeed, be the last bastion of feminist
nilitancy and the only major institution—outside the home—in
vhich women either reign supreme over men, or try to.

In this sense, it could be argued that the YWCA is trailing
:he times, a situation other old-line groups have found themselves in and have remedied as well as they could. A history of
:he needs and interests of young people and how they have
oeen met may be seen, for example, in a fairly elementary study
of merit badges for both Boy and Girl Scouts. The first Girl
Scout Handbook, written by the organization's founder, Juli-
:tte Low, in 1916, offered awards for invalid cooking, cycling,
lairying, laundering, farming, housekeeping, needlework and
"automobiling." A revised handbook issued seven years later
outlined new awards, for beekeeper, business woman, canner,

child nurse, cook, dressmaker, handywoman, home nurse, horse woman, hostess, milliner, driver, star gazer, signaler, driver and rock tapper.

A recent revision of the entire program has brought a new concept of awards, which now have such labels as World Neighbor, My World, My Government, My Community, My Country and Active Citizen. To win a World Neighbor badge, a girl must chart an imaginary trip abroad and study the people, customs, government and history of each country she plans to visit. My World calls also for imaginary trips, extensive reading, a study of a United Nations agency and the planning of a U.N. service project for children. The study of elections and candidates and of how laws are enacted are requirements of the My Government award, with the other civic-oriented badges having comparable tests.

These subjects are a long way from beekeeping or rock tapping—and undoubtedly not nearly so much fun. They also would appear to duplicate much of what Girl Scouts are supposed to be learning in school. This is a kind of duplication that must sometimes confuse youngsters and it certainly removes a considerable amount of the lore from Girl Scouting. Indeed, it may even eliminate the "scouting" from Girl Scouting.

The Boy Scouts have not changed their emphasis so sharply, although they, too, have omitted some of the fun. The earliest Boy Scout badge requirements, set forth in 1911, were for aviation, electricity, camping and cooking. Eight years later, the merit badge for wireless, now called radio, was introduced. To win the aviation award, a Scout was required to have a knowledge of the theory of "aeroplanes," balloons, dirigibles and engines; to make a working model of an aeroplane or dirigible that would fly at least twenty-five yards and to build a box kite that would fly.

Now the award has requirements so complicated they include learning how to read an aeronautical chart; making a pilot's check list for a routine preflight inspection of a light airplane (note change in spelling); building a gasoline-powered model plane that will fly at least fifty seconds; explaining by use of models or illustrations the operation of piston, jet and rocket engines, and learning the instruments on an airplane panel. Nowhere is that original requirement—the one that undoubtedly was the most fun—building and flying a kite.

Don't youngsters do *anything* any more just for fun? Or are they afraid they will be criticized for "wasting" their time? It should be added that it is possible to *learn* something from kite flying as well as to *enjoy* a rare kind of pleasure. Real adventure has been missed by children who have not flown a kite—and that includes Boy Scouts.

In their attempts to keep pace with the times, the Boy and Girl Scouts have found they must develop special programs for older teen-agers to keep them in Scouting. The same conclusions have been reached by other youth groups, including the Camp Fire Girls and the Girls' and Boys' Clubs. One wonders why it took sociologists to make this discovery, but "discover" it they did in a series of expensive surveys.

The Boy Scouts found their solution in the Explorer program for older boys, featuring the study of science and auto mechanics and including trips and cruises. The Girl Scouts, too, have groups for older girls, but more senior members might be retained if they were appointed to lead troops for younger girls, giving mothers now heading troops other tasks.

The daily good deed Scouts have been performing for more than fifty years has been brought up to date. Boy Scouts began their work in 1911 with a national clean-up campaign, a drive for a "safe and sane" Fourth of July and the filling of Thanksgiving and Christmas baskets. Somewhere along the line, they also picked up a tradition that has inspired cartoonists over the decades, namely, helping old ladies to cross streets. The good works of Boy Scouts have been expanded and made more meaningful with programs in safety, conservation and good citizenship. Scouts have planted trees, hedges and grass as well as food shrubs for wildlife, distributed fire-prevention posters and delittered roadsides and parks.

World War II gave the Boy Scouts and all other youth movements their biggest impetus. Youngsters helped on the home front wherever they could and peace found them, along with older groups, casting about for ways to continue serving. The old decided to help the young and the young wanted to help everyone, with the result that probably more litter has been swept up and more trees have been planted than anyone could care to weigh or count.

The Girl Scouts kept up their war-born involvement with blood banks and hospital programs. They added work in libraries and museums, in occupational therapy clinics and in offices of charitable organizations. Their projects are not quite so cut and dried as they used to be, when girls collected for Christmas baskets or made scrapbooks for hospitalized children and did little else. Now they try to be inventive. Members of a troop in Arlington, Virginia, served as aides at the International Center in Washington, providing hospitality for foreigners. New York Scouts expanded a "sidewalk babysitting" service outside the polls on election day to a point where they walked dogs, watched packages, helped old people, made emergency telephone calls and ran errands for election officials.

Less publicized but equally upbeat are the Camp Fire Girls, members of the first national nonsectarian organization in the United States for girls of every race, creed and economic status. Established in 1910 after people started asking when there was going to be a scouting organization for girls, the Camp Fire Girls have clung to their rituals and awards based on Indian lore but have altered requirements. The first manual, a 100-page booklet bound in kraft paper, contained the oath taken by every Camp Fire Girl, who vowed to "seek beauty, give service, pursue knowledge, be trustworthy, hold on to health, glorify work and be happy." In 1942, "worship of God" was added.

The early honors stressed what in 1910 were new standards of hygienic living for women, including sleeping outdoors or with windows open wide during the coldest months of the year and never missing school because of headaches, colds or other minor ills. Girls were required to know the best season to obtain fruits and vegetables and how much to pay for them. Business honors were accorded members who held regular jobs in which they earned enough money to contribute $3 to a "worthy cause" and open savings accounts. Girls who helped clean streets and beautify yards won patriotism awards.

Some of these activities, especially home crafts, became outmoded with advances in food preparation and the introduction of frozen foods. The original Camp Fire Statement of Purposes also has been revised to eliminate concern over standards for women's work and the promotion of community social activities. Labor unions, social action groups and modern industrial management do most of the worrying now about working conditions for women. On the social level, Camp Fire Girls used to provide entertainments and cultural programs in small towns that otherwise would have been intellectually arid. The need for this service has been obviated by radio, television, movies, little theater groups and municipal recreation departments.

Other changes have been effected. Campfires have been turned into cookouts. Daily health charts no longer are regarded as mandatory. The ceremonial Indian gown was made optional after it was learned that many girls did not really want to wear costumes. The study of conservation and literature was dropped, the first because it began to receive nationwide attention and the second because it was introduced in schools. Camp Fire Girls have continued their involvement with conservation programs embracing the planting of millions of trees and the installation of thousands of houses for bluebirds, but there no longer is any originality in such activity.

Conservation is about the first thing a youth group undertakes after it has been organized by a group of adults striving to steer juveniles from becoming delinquent. Such programs often are proposed by grown-up leaders who may be a bit short on imagination. These leaders gradually are awakening to the fact, however, that young people do not want to be categorized as conservationists or performers of childish good deeds. They want to be included in adult programs, or at least to participate in activities that can be considered adult. In short, they want to win recognition as *people,* not as that nice group of young-sters who have been planting trees in the city park.

The Boys' Clubs organization has tried to remedy this situation with a "youth on wheels" driving school in which boys are taught that to own a car is a sign of maturity. They are required to take psychological and mechanical tests, prove that they are safe drivers and help motorists in distress.

Many members are honored every year for their "do-good" Boys' Club spirit, with the grand prize going to the "Boy of the Year, the nation's finest example of juvenile decency." The award usually is presented by one of the most illustrious of the nation's one-time underprivileged boys, former President Herbert Hoover, chairman and chief benefactor of the Boys' Clubs. The 1961 Boy of the Year was 17-year-old Richard Lopez, who lived with his widowed mother and three younger brothers in a poor district in El Paso, who built and painted an addition to the house and washed, ironed and cooked while his mother worked; who held several part-time jobs, but who also found time to be a Junior Joiner par excellence. Richard was presi-dent of his sophomore and junior classes and a member of the Student Council. He was a Future Farmer of America, although he planned to be a lawyer. He played baseball, basketball and tennis, sold rose bushes for the United Fund and Goodwill drives and was chairman of a fund-raising and canned goods drive for the needy. Despite this fragmentation, his studies did not suffer; far from it, Richard was a member of his school's honor society.

He represented that body of teen-agers with so much energy that it appears that belonging to as many clubs as possible may serve as a kind of safety valve. Unspent energies could create only frustrations or lead to misspent hours. It can be argued that organized youth is too busy to get into trouble. But there also is the possibility that they are too involved in *using* time, rather than *investing* it. There is little evidence that the well-intentioned adult molders of youth are encouraging their heirs and successors to learn how to be by themselves, either to think or to create. Everyone must be part of a group or there is something the matter with him, in the view of the arbiters of teen-age society. Actually, the "non organization" youth can be as well oriented as—perhaps even better than—the compulsive joiner in constant pursuit of the security of the group and recognition from his elders.

Rewards are offered generously in every youth group. It is felt necessary to encourage young people by promising a reward for good performance and by instilling a competitive spirit. This is a reflection of adult life. It is supposed to prepare young people to meet the competition of later years, but it certainly must take much of the fun out of being a child, especially of doing something just for the enjoyment of it. Little League baseball, for example, has professionalized the small fry's games to a point where every player is expected to try to emulate Babe Ruth or Roger Maris. The fathers who have organized and supervised the Little Leaguers insist on regulation uniforms, regulation bats and balls, diamonds set up meticulously and close adherence to the rule books. Mothers berate their sons from the sidelines when they strike out or turn butterfingers when trying to catch a fly ball. What goes on at these games is nothing like the fun the neighborhood gang used to have when it played with whatever number of youngsters were available, used stones for bases and let girls join in when team shortages became acute. Sometimes the children did not even keep score. They just played baseball, without the aid—or deterrence—of their parents, for the mere fun of it.

These were "average" youngsters. What becomes of the "average" youngster today, the one who didn't quite make it, the *C* student, the lad who never got past second-class Boy Scout, the girl who liked to camp but thought fires should be built by boys? Has anyone ever made a study of what happens to the average boy and girl when they grow up, beyond the fact that they have "X" dollars in the bank, "X.2" children and at least one TV set per household? It is possible, of course, that the *average* youngster is the one who got the most out of the activities in which he engaged, because he got just what *he* wanted out of them, not what the standard-setters, test-givers and leaders thought he should. He did not try to measure up to anything except his own interests. One of the busy sociologists peering into the behavior patterns of Americans ought to pry into the mind of the one-time "average" child. He might discover that the kid no one noticed remembers today more of what he learned in Troop 5 than the Eagle Scout who felt compelled to win every badge in the book.

It is a tribute to youthful tenacity and stamina that so many teen-agers who stand at the tops of their classes scholastically are among the most ardent joiners. One wonders whether more of the energy and interest of young people might be channeled into school work instead of extracurricular matters if the opportunities for *learning* equaled those for *joining*. While it is true that joining is part of a search—or perhaps a groping—for new interests and career choices, there is the possiblity that this quest lacks organization because of a profusion of organizations. Young people are reaching into a grabbag of gregariousness, and it may turn out that their reach is indeed greater than their grasp.

.11.

Project Youth

THE ORGANIZATION YOUTH NOT ONLY HAS PROJECTS—HE IS a project. Adult groups dedicated to good works have made service to young people one of their major contributions to society and to their own feelings of satisfaction over being "useful." Recognizing the penchant of young people for being joiners, the adults have provided them with a wide choice of organizations that serve youth and encourage them, in turn, to be of service, setting off chain reactions of good deeds that often keep whole communities humming with activity.

Teen-agers have found friends in adult groups, so many that it sometimes seems that youngsters may be in danger of being killed with the kindness of all the programs in their behalf. Such groups as the Optimists, Kiwanis, Rotary, Elks, Moose, American Legion and Daughters of the American Revolution have provided so many activities, often with duplicating or overlapping programs, that a young person who is involved in more than one—and thousands are—must lead a fragmented life.

Just about every organization that makes youth its project rewards youngsters with medals, trophies, certificates, money or scholarships. Some groups honor thousands of young people every year in local, state and national competitions to select the best leader, the smartest student, the most able orator, the

117

girl who can sew the straightest seam or the boy most likely to fly to the moon.

Days, weeks and months are set aside to honor youth. Optimist International, "friend of the boy," has an Annual Youth Appreciation Week, while the Kiwanis Clubs, under the slogan of "Youth serves youth," hold an annual Kids' Day. Rotary stages a Boys' and Girls' Week; the Elks, a Youth Day, and the Moose, a Youth Honor Day. The Lions Clubs have a Youth Week and a Career Day. The American Legion outdoes them all with a Boys' and Girls' Week, an American Education Week and a Citizenship Day.

One boy or girl VIP may be a winner or finalist in several contests and be active in every youth day or week that comes along. So numerous are the events that one wonders if it might not be more efficient and effective—and be of more help to youth—if all the groups were to get together and stage a few mammoth annual nationwide youth observances instead of scattering their fire and vying for attention for themselves and their separate programs. Much of the money that has been poured into duplicating efforts could be made available for acutely needed scholarships or other benefits more vital than parade costumes or colorful posters. Well-organized national service projects could have a greater impact in the organizations' avowed efforts to convince adults that the youngsters really are not too bad after all.

The Optimists, founded more than forty years ago for fellowship and service, began their Youth Appreciation Week in 1957 as a result of the success of a local observance in Charlotte, North Carolina, where Optimist members, weary of often careless criticism of youth, decided to do something to boost the morale of "the responsible 95 per cent." They staged a weeklong festival honoring the nonbeat generation. Now more than 1,000,000 youngsters are involved in the International Optimist Youth Appreciation Week and nearly 30,000 are individually honored at rallies, club meetings devoted to youth, "mayor-for-a-day" programs, spelling bees and safe-driving demonstrations. The slogan "Pat 'em on the back" is pasted on auto bumpers, emblazoned on billboards and blared from radio and television speakers.

"Youth serves youth" is the theme of the Kiwanis Kids' Day, which in 1961 had a slogan imploring, "Give our youth a crash kit of essentials." The day, begun in 1948 as a "kickoff" for making every day Kids' Day, features all manner of events honoring young people as the "hope for the future."

"Give the kids entertainment, of course, but give them something, too, that will stay with them in the years to come," Kiwanis says. "Give them the feeling that they are appreciated; give them the opportunity to express their own creativeness; give them something that will make them more aware of their approaching responsibilities as citizens in a free democracy."

While the Kiwanis honors youth in September, the Elks chose May 1, to compete with the traditional May Day demonstrations of left-wing groups. The Elks Leadership Contest was begun in 1950, with Youth Day being inaugurated the following year. Each local lodge finds its own way to recognize youth, but the principal activity of most at the outset was the "mayor-for-a-day" program, now considered something of a cliché in the youth field. Elk programs soon began to take on more substance, with hobby shows and recreational activities calling for some ingenuity. The occasion has been growing less social and more educational; many state groups now emphasize college scholarship awards in response to critics who feared that there was a danger of making the programs too trivial or mere gestures attracting more attention to the Elks than to the youngsters they sought to help.

October 31 is set aside each year by the Loyal Order of Moose for its Youth Honor Day, the main object of which is to obtain signed pledges from as many youngsters as possible promising to refrain from "defacing, mutilating or destroying property or performing any act harmful to others during the Hallowe'en season." The Moose began the observance because it felt that there should be a Youth Day, just as there are

Mother's and Father's Days, and Hallowe'en seemed to them an ideal occasion both to make teen-agers feel important and to convince them that squashing overripe tomatoes on front doors and dumping the contents of garbage cans on lawns were not the thing to do. "Trick-or-treat" has given way on the Moose agenda to circuses, carnivals, minstrel shows, outings, picnics, parades, rodeos and excursions. Planning for the occasion begins in August, and the Moose recommend that it be a community-wide project, thus keeping many adults busy for three months thinking of ways to thwart youthful pranksters from doing what their parents got away with a generation ago without even so much as a hint that they might wind up in Sing Sing as a result.

The inevitable awards on the despooked Hallowe'en go to winners of contests in decorating store windows artistically instead of with wax or soap, costume designing, essay writing and float construction. A feature devised to outploy would-be mischief-makers is a "fireside contest" in which prizes are given to children found at home when telephoned at random on Hallowe'en night. Such an evening of forced boredom is all right with the few youngsters who win, but the others are left with their virtue unrewarded.

Essays, oratory, scholarship, citizenship and marksmanship are among the skills recognized by the American Legion in its extensive Americanism program. November 11, formerly Armistice Day and now Veterans' Day, is the focal point of American Education Week, founded in 1921 by the Legion and the National Education Association, with the later enlistment of the United States Office of Education and the National Congress of Parents and Teachers, to familiarize adults with school problems and progress. Some of the prize-winning youngsters receive certificates of distinguished achievement, while others are given medals or plaques.

A National High School Oratorical Contest is conducted by the Legion every April, each department offering at least one local scholarship. Begun in 1938, the contest now attracts more than 350,000 students, with the national winner receiving a $4,000 scholarship and runners-up scholarships of $2,500, $1,000 and $500.

The Legion sponsors two popular civic programs—Boys' State and Boys' Nation—in which boys gather every year to establish mock governmental units ranging from city to nation in scope. In these sessions, usually held on college or university campuses, boys form political parties, stage elections and then legislate and govern the units to which they belong. Girls are included at the county government level.

Youth work is regarded by Rotarians as their "long-term investment in the future." Their first Boys' and Girls' Week was held in New York City. Now it is a national event. Rotarians lend money to students, provide scholarships and give many awards, including one that is unique in that it rewards *effort* rather than *excellence*. This honor is given by the Tyndall, South Dakota, Rotary Club to the boy and girl showing the greatest improvement in high school.

Service to young people by adult organizations often goes far beyond doing them honor. The grown-ups are leading sponsors of Boy Scout, Girl Scout and Camp Fire Girl troops. Rotary is the largest single sponsor of Boy Scout groups; the American Legion sponsors a number also. Many 4-H clubs and career planning organizations are adult projects. Safety, traffic control and conservation are favorite projects of nearly every program organized by adults for children. Here, again, coordination might provide greater significance and a larger contribution to the nation. An over-all plan, with each organization assigned a job and a place in which to perform it might be more meaningful than a hodgepodge of token street-crossing programs here and tree-planting campaigns there. An anti-litter drive in Keokuk may make that town tidy and cause the older folks to sit up and take notice of youth, but why not extend the effort to Kenosha and Kennebunkport, too?

No organization is more active in trying to serve the community by serving youth than the Optimists, at the outset "friend of the *delinquent* boy," and now friend of all boys. Many of their youth projects are local, as in Bala Cynwyd, a suburb of Philadelphia, where Optimists assumed sponsorship of youngsters who formed a club to try to remove the "stigma of being teen-agers" after one of them had been arrested falsely during a crackdown on juvenile loitering. The San Leandro, California, Junior Optimist Rifle Club received help from its adult sponsors in transforming a garbage dump into a rifle range and clubhouse where 450 young people receive instruction in safe hunting techniques. An electronics school for boys has been the youth project of Optimists in Greenville, Tennessee.

Optimists work through clubs with headquarters off school grounds, but Kiwanians are associated closely with schools in their youth projects. They have organized Key Clubs as service groups for boys in the tenth to twelfth grades and Circle K Clubs for college men. The Key Clubs operate under school regulations but are counseled by business and professional men. The more than 1,800 clubs meet weekly, usually for lunch, and perform such civic services as organizing teen-age community recreation centers, operating car-wash laundries and supervising patriotic programs and Savings Bond drives. Within the school, Key Club members campaign against vandalism and promote good sportsmanship. They present vocational guidance programs, operate safety patrols and have been known to volunteer suggestions for improving textbooks. One rather unromantic "civic contribution" by a Key Club was a campaign to halt the carving of initials on trees.

Fund-raising projects sometimes reflect a certain degree of youthful ingenuity, such as selling a Key Club member at auction to serve as a slave to the highest bidder for an hour or buying an old auto wreck and letting students vent steam by smiting it with a sledgehammer at 25 cents a whack. One club conducted an "ugliest man" contest for 10 cents a vote.

Key Club members have recruited blood donors, circulated election petitions, swept school auditoriums, cleaned water fountains and painted traffic lines on streets. At Roosevelt High, in Atlanta, they organized a lost-and-found service that gave unclaimed clothing to the needy and auctioned other items for a student fund. Members in Fox Valley, Georgia, located abandoned refrigerators, which are hazardous to small children, and persuaded owners to remove the doors. When a hurricane hit southeastern Louisiana, Key Club members at LaGrange Senior High School in Lake Charles manned small boats to rescue survivors and recover bodies.

The charter Key Club was founded in Sacramento, California, in 1925. Twenty-two years later the first Circle K group was formed at Carthage College, in Illinois. The new group became an international organization only in 1956, building its program on the usual range of projects involving safety, entertainment for underprivileged children and scholarships for needy students. Circle K members also tutor other students and publish campus directories and song books. They are regarded as Big Men on Campus at the University of Jacksonville, in Florida, and Dr. Weimer K. Hicks, president of Kalamazoo College, in Michigan, says Circle K is an important addition to the campus, which is "pregnant with the need and desire for service clubs."

"These young men, tomorrow's leaders," says Hicks, "are serious beyond their years. A divided and insecure world has made them that way. They want the challenge that Circle K presents. Have no fears. They will not disappoint us."

Nor, it is to be hoped, will they disappoint themselves or find disappointment in the ways in which elders have guided them. The goals of quite a few of the groups that have involved themselves with youth often seem to be aimed less at actually doing something for or with youth than at putting young people to work for an organization or a cause.

The Daughters of the American Revolution, pillar of patriotic self-righteousness, has developed an extensive education program with a broad accent on Americanism. More than $450,000 in DAR funds goes into education every year, including the support of two schools in the Southern mountains. The organization estimates that it reaches about 9,000 young persons a year with student loans and scholarships. It also presents many hundreds of "good citizen" awards through 5,500 Junior American Citizen Clubs, with 253,000 members who enroll in courses in courtesy, history and American culture and conduct campaigns in—you guessed it—safety and conservation.

Disasters, personal and general, are the missions of the Junior Red Cross and its 20,000,000 members, who stand ready to serve in fire, flood or auto accident. No mishap is too large or too small for this army of young people trained in disaster relief, artificial respiration and the application of tourniquets. The Junor Red Cross was organized in 1917 to roll bandages for World War I casualties. It has been busy ever since, in first aid, home nursing, water safety and flood and hurricane aid in peacetime, and blood campaigns, bandage-rolling and fund-raising in wartime.

Some Red Cross chapters are doing what other adult groups have neglected to do—namely, giving young people grown-up roles and a chance to work *with*, not *for*, adults. A special leadership training program is available to the more able youngsters and they help formulate policies as well as direct their own activities. The Hinds-Rankin Counties Red Cross Youth Council in Jackson, Mississippi, for example, organized its own disaster preparedness unit, which is ready to go into action when trouble strikes.

The programs described here represent but a sampling of the adult-youth projects in progress. All of these adult-conceived-and-directed activities are designed to give young people a sense of importance and discourage a feeling that they exist in a limbo in which they are neither children nor adults. The activities are aimed also at encouraging young people to participate in civic affairs after they grow up. Whether giving them their "day" or "week" or "month" and medals, certificates and plaques really offers a permanent impetus may be questioned, but it cannot be gainsaid that there are momentary pleasures, which are demonstrated by the enthusiasm with which young people participate in any activity where they are the center of attention —or a least can share the spotlight with others.

The adults who have made young people their projects are equally enthusiastic and sometimes equally desirous, at least subconsciously, of being noticed. Many are parents—fathers who otherwise would be buried in newspapers or staring at television in the evening and mothers seeking to be "useful" in the free time afforded by their automated kitchens. The busyness of their children can be contagious. Whether the result is a time filler or time user for an adult varies according to the individual. Some parents, unfortunately, are no more suited to guiding other people's children than their own and make poor leaders. Indeed, the childless adult often may be a much better counselor. Out of the whole maze of activities in which adults make children their projects, one key question arises: Who benefits most from Project Youth, the adults or the children?

.12.

Futures Unlimited

ONCE UPON A TIME WHEN A LITTLE BOY WAS ASKED WHAT he was going to be when he grew up, he unhesitatingly declared that he wanted to be a fireman, policeman, milkman or iceman, or possibly Hopalong Cassidy or a railroad engineer. His choice varied from day to day, but the range was limited and the goal was reasonably modest.

There once was a game played by little girls in which they counted off buttons, beads or flower petals with a chant that went something like this—"rich man, poor man, beggar man, thief, doctor, lawyer, merchant chief." Whichever name fell on the last button, bead or petal identified the "profession" of the man a little girl would marry when she grew up.

If there is such a game today, the choices must be different. Somehow, multi-millionaire, minister, physicist, space man and jet pilot would have to fit into little girls' dreams of the future, judging from the ambitions of little boys.

Youngsters are keeping up with the times—or at least with television's version of the times—just like everyone else, and their heroes depend in large part on who is this week's TV idol. Gone are those one-time heroes of children—those two strong and smiling daily callers, the iceman and the milkman, career ideals of very small fry in the pre-electronic era. Today, no one would think of casting either of them as heroes on television—there is a strong chance, in fact, that most younger children do not even know what an iceman is.

Cowboys may still offer a certain inspiration to youngsters via the medium of the flickering tube, but if a boy today says he is going to be on the police force when he grows up, he means he is going to be J. Edgar Hoover or Eliot Ness. He wants to be Jonas Salk, Commander Alan B. Shepard Jr. or John F. Kennedy, not an iceman or a deliverer of milk.

Many former idols have fallen. Medical specialization has reduced the ranks of old-fashioned family doctors who treated everyone in a household and listened to their troubles while he was about it. With the development of specialists and hospitalization insurance policies that minimize treatment at home, there are fewer opportunities for the kind of intimacy between doctor and patient that prompted many a boy to say he wanted to be a doctor just like his doctor when he grew up. Sights today are set on other and rather impersonal, often lonely, goals—laboratory benches, supersonic jets and rockets to the moon—and they are set at increasingly younger ages because there is so much to learn and such a short time in which to learn it.

Children start talking career with more than a childish air almost as soon as they enter their first schoolroom—and their parents start saving for the day when they will be called upon to finance an expensive education that may continue for years and produce two or three college degrees. "Plan ahead" has become an unwritten law in education and it can mean beginning in kindergarten. In a new "K-through-12" (kindergarten through high school) program, for example, science is being taught in many public schools along with the ABC's. It has indeed become the "fourth r," in addition to readin', 'ritin' and 'rithmatic. Languages also are being introduced in grade schools. Specialization is being urged as early as the interest of a youngster can be attracted. The most emphatic bids are being made at the high school level, but the time may come when teachers' groups, scientists and medical schools start scouting among grade school students, because the competition for the gifted students—the most talented and brightest—is growing fiercer all the time.

Vocational guidance counselors are busy in high schools as well as colleges trying to help young people find the right careers, and trying to help the careers find the right young people. At the elbows of the advisers stand the organizers of the wide array of "career" organizations covering just about every "future" occupation one could name except perhaps "future mothers."

Shortages abound in many professions, among them engineering, medicine and the law. There never are enough chemists and skilled craftsmen. The shortage of teachers is alarming even though increasing numbers of young people are entering the profession and a good many persons have switched to education from other occupations. Into a jumble of conflicting demands comes the career club, the career guidance counselor, the career conference. The Junior Joiners who sometimes find themselves in several career clubs at once become objects of a game of tug-of-war. They are told there are more than 40,000 job titles in the United States and that they must choose among them. The Department of Labor reports that there now are more white-collar than blue-collar jobs and that educational requirements for all good positions are increasing. It is an established fact that the higher the education, the greater the average earning potential.

Many young men find career guidance in the armed forces, where they are given specialized training they can carry back to civilian life. A few are fortunate enough to have developed a talent early and received the proper encouragement, so they do not have to make a choice. Most apparently take pot luck, drifting into their life's work despite all the help being offered. However, youngsters are beginning to ask what jobs are available in their communities, how much they pay, whether there are opportunities for advancement and whether there are "fringe benefits." They want to know the disadvantages, too.

Mainly they want to find work that is rewarding in ways beyond the financial.

Businessmen have been trying to ease the shortage of technically trained manpower by arranging work-study programs for students, sponsoring fellowships and scholarships in science and engineering and paying the tuition of employees to take advanced technical courses. They are giving old laboratory equipment to schools, opening plants for student tours and hiring high school science teachers for summer and part-time jobs.

The United States Chamber of Commerce encourages career conferences for teen-agers, particularly in the hope of halting the heavy rate of drop-outs from high school, which is estimated to be as high as 40 per cent in some cities and is reported to include many gifted young people who are not being challenged. The Chamber wants young people to have more information and advice on job opportunities and requirements. It recommends psychological testing of abilities, aptitudes and interests, and the counsel of experts, such as businessmen and professional specialists.

The career conference, which has been found generally useful, usually features an assembly with a speaker discussing career selection in general terms. This is followed by group discussions of specific vocations. Under Chamber auspices, students have attended conferences in Lufkin, Texas, on careers in business, radio and television and fashion modeling. The Davenport, Iowa, Chamber coordinated with the Board of Education to provide an accountant and radio-TV experts to explain the opportunities in their fields.

A "boss-for-a-day" job-evaluation program is conducted by the Miami Beach Chamber of Commerce, while various other Chambers sponsor student work-study programs, summer jobs and career seminars. Another local career exploration is offered in Santa Barbara County, California, where high school students work in local business and industry as part of their senior study program. A student begins as an observer, without pay but with school credits. Then he works part-time as a clerk, messenger or sales assistant, receiving both pay and credit. More important vocational assignments come later, still involving pay as well as credit.

The Junior Chamber of Commerce, itself a young man's organization, has formed the Jaybees—the Junior Business Bureau—for high school boys. Begun in Pensacola, Florida, in 1956 to counter cries of "J.D.," the bureau tries to foster interest in both business careers and civic betterment along with promoting Juvenile Decency. A Young Adult Placement Program, described as "America's blueprint for the future," is provided by the Jaycees, who urge adults to let boys and girls choose their occupations after hearing what the grown-ups have to say. The Junior Chambers make up lists of the jobs most frequently sought after and most often available and try to do missionary work among employers to convince them that gainful occupations make young people more useful citizens and that often youngsters work harder and for less money and learn more, faster than persons twice their age. "We hire the handicapped, so why not the young adult?" the Jaycees ask.

The Jaycees, 200,000 "young men of action . . . the broadest base of stockholders in the future of the United States," range from 21 through 35 years of age and have been trying to prove since their founding in the early 1920's that young men *can* change the world. They already have proved that the world changes the young man's standards for success; their barometer is the annual selection of "The Ten Outstanding Young Men of America." The ten are chosen as examples of the opportunities available in the free-enterprise system. Since the first group was namd in 1938, the kind of men chosen has changed quite a bit. In the early days, the judges leaned heavily toward athletes and entertainers. Today—more than 200 outstanding young men later—athletes sometimes are chosen, but scientists and other intellectuals prevail. When Pat Boone was included on a recent list, it was as much for his authorship of books to help teen-agers and his church leadership as for his spectacular singing career.

A glance at the first list and one of the most recent shows how times have changed for young men. Those who made the list in 1938 were:

> *Howard Hughes,* millionaire movie-maker and airplane manufacturer.
> *George Gallup,* poll-taker.
> *Orson Welles,* precocious actor-director.
> *Rudy Vallee,* crooner.
> *Elmer F. Layden,* coach of the Notre Dame football team.
> *Douglas Corrigan,* who flew to fame by crossing the Atlantic the wrong way.
> *William McChesney Martin Jr.,* at 32 president of the New York Stock Exchange.
> *Louis Adamic,* writer.
> *Paul C. Smith,* public-relations counsel to former President Herbert Hoover.
> *Philip C. Ebeling,* president of the Jaycees.

All were in their 30's except Welles, who was 23. Adamic, at 39, was the oldest.

The 1961 list was heavily weighted with eggheads who were not so easy to identify as the 1938 choices. They were:

> *MacCarter Adams, Ph.D.,* research scientist who helped make the re-entry of an intercontinental ballistics missile (ICBM) possible.
> *Robert A. Bicks,* who at 33 was the youngest man ever to be Assistant Attorney General of the United States.
> *Doyle E. Conner,* Florida's Commissioner of Agriculture.
> *Richard L. Garwin, Ph.D.,* physicist and associate director of IBM's Watson Laboratory.
> *Rafer L. Johnson,* Negro who set an Olympic Games decathalon record.
> *George Cabot Lodge,* Assistant Secretary of Labor for International Affairs in the Eisenhower Administration and son of Henry Cabot Lodge.
> *Harry W. Morgan,* special assistant to the president of Macalester College and a pioneer in "people-to-people" democracy.
> *John H. Nelson,* Atlanta Constitution reporter and Pulitzer Prize winner.
> *Robert S. Schwartz, M.D.,* who found a new approach to the

treatment of disease through his study of antibody reaction in kidney transplant operations.

Don Walsh, Navy explorer who made a record-breaking plunge of nearly seven miles off Guam in a bathyscaph.

Three of these young men—Johnson, Morgan and Walsh— were in their 20's. The oldest, at 36, was Adams.

While the first list seemed to favor the big moneymakers and the spectacular successes, the later one drew heavily on accomplishments that are not likely to bring riches and may not make the largest headlines. The selections show a trend toward finding success in the laboratory, a situation that has given pause to many youngsters with neither the talent nor inclination to seek scientific careers. A young man decides he will be a history major in college. "What for?" people ask. "There is no future in it, no money." That is what people asked not too long ago when a boy abandoned a baseball bat for a slide rule. Today the nuclear scientist is our authority on "everything." Perhaps in another ten or twenty years the historian will be lionized as the only person qualified to tell us where we went wrong.

Even the farmer may have a future equal to his past. Right now, however, farming is "bombsville" as far as young people are concerned. It has become increasingly difficult to keep them down on the farm, whether they have seen Paree or not. To confuse the picture, city folk increasingly are moving to rural areas —fashionably called exurbia. This situation has brought a change in one of the oldest and most firmly established youth programs—the Four-H Clubs. During most of its more than fifty years of teaching young people how to milk cows and candle eggs, under the guidance of the Department of Agriculture's Extension Service, 4-H (Head, Heart, Hands and Health to better living) has grown to more than 2,300,000 members and 21,300,000 alumni with a program that has been adapted to suit urbanites as well as exurbanites. Leaders of 4-H know that most of the young people they serve will go into nonfarm work but that 40 per cent of all jobs are in some way related to agriculture, so a knowledge of farming can still be useful.

Various 4-H groups study the science of weather, nutrition and insect control. They learn the proper care and use of electrical equipment and cultivate vegetable gardens.

The other major farm organization for youth, Future Farmers of America, limits its membership mainly to young people who plan to make careers of farming. They must at least be enrolled in vocational classes in agriculture in high school. The federally aided FFA program offers training in the techniques and science of agricultural production all the way from planting to the market. The organization, with 380,000 active members, is an offshoot of the apprentice systems of former times. Members advance from Greenhand through Chapter Farmer, State Farmer and American Farmer ratings. Awards are given for farm mechanics, electrification, soil and water management, dairy farming and safety.

While farm leaders fight a drift to the cities, educators have to battle against the lure of higher paying and sometimes more personally rewarding fields than teaching. Although the number of persons going into teaching is up, it is not high enough. Recent college graduating classes provided a total of 85,000 teachers to fill 220,000 openings. One organization dedicated to trying to remedy this situation is the Future Teachers of America. Sponsored by the National Education Association, the FTA tries to help develop effective recruiting programs in which capable candidates are found and interested in teaching. It apparently is meeting with some success, for in the 1960 annual scholarship contest of NEA's National Honor Society, teaching was listed as the leading career choice of the highest-ranking senior participants.

It is the undecided percentage that various career groups are aiming at, and none is trying harder than the Future Scientists of America, also sponsored by a division of NEA. Another NEA affiliate fosters the Future Business Leaders of America, which grew from one club with seventy-two members in 1937 to 3,000 clubs with 76,000 members in 1957.

Future nurses' groups are trying to fill serious shortages by encouraging high school girls to work as hospital aides and in other tasks they can perform in order to appraise the possibilities of careers in the medical world. Most of the clubs have been formed since 1950 under the sponsorship of the National League for Nursing. A recent study showed that 25 per cent of today's student nurses chose their career before they were ten years old. This means that it is to the older girl that the league must make its appeal.

For girls, homemaking is a career that requires training. It no longer is fashionable for a girl to enter marriage bragging that she cannot boil water. The bride who knows nothing about cooking is a rarity, but the Future Homemakers of America, sponsored by the American Home Economics Association and the Home Economics Education Branch of the United States Office of Education, wants her to know more than mere fundamentals. The FHA offers programs for training high school students in the fine points of homemaking, such as budgeting time and money, preparing meals on short notice, remodeling clothes and learning how to deal with the intricacies of human relationships within the family.

Homemaking has become such a science that the FHA hopes that tomorrow's bride will not bog down in a dull routine and find herself telling people, "Oh, I'm *only* a housewife." If the FHA has its way, the word "housewife" will go the way of the icebox.

"Future unlimited" is the slogan of a dynamic and fast-growing "career" group called Junior Achievement. Founded several decades ago as a "learning-by-doing" program in Springfield, Massachusetts, it did not really start moving until after World War II and now reports more than 80,000 teen-agers working in 4,500 miniature companies organized each year. Junior Achievement offers high school students a chance for practical experience in establishing and operating small businesses with expert adult guidance but never direction. The youngsters sell stock and manufacture and market products or services. The merchandise has included earrings and television sets, chairs and barbecue grills. One company produced radio and television shows. Another published a city directory containing profitable advertising. Stock is sold for 50 cents a share, with a limit of five shares to any investor. The average capitalization is about $100, the average gross sales are about $300.

Junior Achievement helps familiarize young people with the free-enterprise system and is an aid in career selection. Some adult sponsors have hired members of the companies after they finished school. The New York Stock Exchange gives a plaque and a trip to New York each year to the officers of the two Junior Achievement companies with the best annual reports.

Quite a few success stories have come out of Junior Achievement. Eugene Gilbert started his now highly successful teen-survey method while a high school student. After he left college, he established a research concern that now is the biggest in the field of taking the pulse of young consumers. Being president of a Chicago Junior Achievement company led James Kappellas to start his own ice cream business. Adrene Terfler of Chicago began her business career with Junior Achievement at the age of 16 and then helped her father start a new business, American Builders Supply Company, for which she supervises promotion, sales and product selection.

Junior Achievement taught Jerry Feldman of St. Louis that "you can't start planning for the future too soon." He began by installing a soft-drink machine in a Junior Achievement center, later adding a candy machine. Two years later, he installed thirty-two machines in St. Louis and then branched out to establish a dry goods and men's furnishings department in his father's limping grocery store and to set up a lawn-mowing business with two college boys as his employees. Later he added a magazine subscription business employing a dozen teen-agers.

A refreshing approach to teen-agers is offered by Junior Achievement and other career groups. Not only is the young person sincerely sought for what *he* can contribute; he is treated as an adult and, at the same time, challenged as a youth. Youngsters in Junior Achievement and some of the other career groups get big problems to solve. Most of the activities are coeducational, with full equality of the sexes.

Nearly every major corporation participates in Junior Achievement. Many offer on-the-job training to the more promising young Achievers. The budding tycoons often find they can teach adults something, too. A survey showed that 75 per cent of the adults who had bought shares in JA companies never owned stock before. The success of their tiny investments often whetted their interest so much that they bought into blue-chip companies on Wall Street.

Other organizations interested in youth might learn something from the newer career groups. The main area in which the career organizations are most attractive to young people is the minimizing of adult supervision to a point where, in many cases, grown-up experts are available whenever their help is needed but otherwise leave the youngsters alone to succeed or fail on their own. This is particularly true of Junior Achievement; when a company gets into trouble it seeks its own way out. Failure sometimes is even regarded as success because it teaches young people a lesson they will not soon forget.

The career groups are unique in offering a single-minded approach to constructive use of leisure time. While Scouting or "Y" work provide broad ranges of busyness, the Future Teachers or Future Scientists are interested in one subject only.

One problem does arise within the "future" groups. Too many youngsters belong to too many of these clubs. They seem to be going off in several directions at once. The high school guidance counselors could step in here and try to intensify their efforts to help students appraise their potentialities and interests more closely. It might be even more to the point if the "future" clubs were to limit membership to those with a talent or interest in the field involved. This could result in the more successful channeling of the right young persons into the right careers.

.13.

There Is Nothing
Dull About Jack

Y OUNG PEOPLE ARE INDUSTRIOUSLY DISPROVING THE OLD
saying that "all work and no play makes Jack a dull boy." They
may indeed be proving the opposite in an age where everyone
must be busy or watch the world pass by. Growing numbers of
youngsters are working, with or without pay, in school and out,
almost the year around, and one could hardly call them dull.
The dullards are more likely to be found among the diminishing
ranks of young people who think weekends and summers are for
unalloyed fun. They do not realize there is no time any more
for that.

Summers are filled with a number of things for scholarly,
industrious or social-minded young people—more every year,
but never enough. When schools let out in June, there is a
stampede for paying summer jobs, service projects—and more
school. A movement is afoot to put schools and colleges on a
year-round basis, but many students are a step ahead of the educators. Serious young people are cushioning themselves against
the educational pressures of the post-sputnik era by studying on
weekends and during summers on their own initiative. They are
not waiting for Vice Admiral Hyman G. Rickover or Dr. James
Bryant Conant to tell them what to do.

In the days before the first Soviet satellite put American edu-

cators into frenzied orbit, summer schools were conducted
mainly for those who needed to make up for lost grades; at least
they were about the only students to report for off-season classes
This is not true any more. Youngsters who flunk subjects stil
enroll in summer school, but so do the brighter students, and in
growing numbers, to take courses they do not have time for in
the regular school year or to elude the boredom of a summer
in which there otherwise would be nothing to do. A shortage of
vacation jobs in recent summers has motivated many young
people to go to summer school; the prosperity of their parent
has helped, too. Some exceptional pupils are so interested in
summer study that they enlist in activities for which they get no
official credit; and they continue their participation on week
ends during the school year.

Travel also has taken on an educational flavor. Young people
seem to feel a sense of guilt if they fritter away their leisure on
the usual frivolities of tourism, so they are participating in
creasingly in travel seminars, studying as they move about, or
attending summer sessions abroad.

The demand for employment that offers no pay or even
requires payment from—instead of to—young workers also is
large. Many more applicants are turned down than are accepted
by those in charge of both paying and nonpaying summer occupations. Teen-agers are the largest body of unemployed persons
in the country—including the group over 65—but not out of
choice. A large proportion of young people would rather do
something useful with their summers than loll on beaches or
loaf on tennis courts. Too many of them have no choice despite
the fact that the government, churches, schools and various
agencies and organizations offer constructive summer activities
for young people. The major drawback lies in the fact that the
opportunities number in the thousands, when millions are
needed.

Examples of summer projects abound, but always for limited
numbers of young people—often for only a handful. Most are
church-related, because religious organizations are almost

unique in having the machinery to find places where help is needed and to send the young people to fill the needs. Church groups are national and even international in scope but they never have the funds to answer all the calls for help.

The Youth Department of the World Council of Churches sponsors work overseas every summer. In 1961, it provided non-paying employment for more than a thousand young people, only a fraction of them Americans, who dug foundations or laid bricks for schools, houses, chapels and refugee centers in thirty-seven countries. Men and women from 18 to 30 built roads, planted trees and helped distribute relief materials.

A "volunteers abroad" summer program is conducted by the National YWCA, which recruits camp counselors and program assistants to buy their own tickets to travel to YWCA branches in Latin America and the Middle East. One of the organization's recent foreign projects was a joint American-Liberian work camp in Sinoe, Liberia.

More modest foreign service projects also are open. One such program was conducted by the Southwest Texas Conference of The Methodist Church, which sent a token task force of four boys and two adults to work in Bolivia for eight weeks. Another small group was financed by the Central Texas Conference to make a study tour of missions of South America.

These are well-publicized programs—possibly overly publicized, considering they are but tokens. They grow more numerous and more extensive each year as increasing funds are made available, but it will be many summers before the desires of youth for summer service abroad are met.

There is a summer task, however small it may be, to fit the abilities, aims and limitations of almost any young person who does not leave home. Such a youngster can participate in a wide variety of community service projects, whether instructing in daily vacation Bible school, teaching Puerto Rican mothers to read or sew, operating day camps or serving in hospitals or the offices of social agencies. The Junior Red Cross offers opportunities for volunteer work in Veterans Administration hospitals,

blood banks and playgrounds in its "summer of service" pro
grams. Other agencies have similar assignments for young
people.

None of these activities involves wages, but it is possible fo
the youngster who cannot find a paying summer job to lear
from volunteer activity. Mention of it always makes an impres
sion in applying for a full-time job later; employers look favor
ably on young people who have been willing to give something
to their communities and can show that they have no objection
to hard work.

There are summer service posts that pay, although moder
ately. The government has internships for able college student
who work in Washington offices in regular jobs giving then
experience and a chance to decide whether they want career
in the Civil Service. The pay seldom is more than enough to
defray the expenses of living in Washington but the jobs give
experience in nearly any field one might choose. The Depart
ment of Agriculture employs students to work in national for
ests and experimental stations. Jobs on highway survey and
construction projects are offered by the Bureau of Public Road
of the Department of Commerce. Semi-professional positions in
biology and the physical sciences are available at Public Health
Service installations, and most Veterans Administration hospi
tals have summer openings.

The YMCA and YWCA cooperate in supervising an annua
Washington Student Citizenship Seminar for six weeks, during
which thirty-five college men and women work in government
agencies and participate in seminars and field trips. Here, again
the openings are severely limited.

A total of only twenty men and women students is hired fo
YMCA-supervised service in social agencies in Seattle, Washing
ton. Slightly more than that number of women students gather
in New York City each year, under YWCA guidance, to work in
social agencies and live in a settlement house where they hold
seminars on the problems of city life and how religious group
can try to solve them.

Independent so-called "do-good" projects are numerous at the local level. They may be church-sponsored or conducted by civic groups. One example of a program developed by youngsters themselves may be found in Philadelphia and its suburbs, where thousands of junior and senior high school students engage in summer programs of community service in an organization called Student Volunteers, which was formed shortly after World War II. The youngsters help in hospitals, libraries, health and welfare agencies, child care centers and playgrounds. Most of the volunteers indicated they had become involved because they could not find paying summer jobs but did not want to sacrifice their summers to inactivity.

This is the heart of one of the biggest problems confronting youth, particularly teen-agers. Summer vacations are too long to devote to just having fun. The old swimming hole holds no attraction for the industrious Twentieth Century boy and girl. Unless schools operate on a year-round basis, as some persons want them to, communities will have to give some thought to helping youngsters put their summers to good use.

It is doubtful that summer schools could handle any more students than they have been receiving. Most teachers take vacations, leaving only skeleton staffs to meet with sharply limited classes in which serious students seek specialized knowledge, largely in foreign languages, international affairs, mathematics and science.

An example of the programs available is found in the Neshaminy School District in Pennsylvania, where courses are offered in the summer in electronics and quantitative analysis, with a class also in oil painting. "Interest centers" are featured in the Winnetka, Illinois, elementary summer sessions, where children study science, drama, mathematics, the arts and languages on more informal and individual bases than during regular sessions. Harvard students preparing to teach serve as interns in a summer program in the Newton, Massachusetts, schools. In Seattle, Washington, grade school pupils may study

French, German, Japanese, Norwegian, Spanish or literature in the summer.

The National Science Foundation sponsors more than 150 local summer training programs for secondary school students with high ability. One of these was a no-tuition course in astronomy and space science at the American Museum-Hayden Planetarium in New York. The class met three mornings a week for lectures on subjects such as "the use of nuclear emulsions in the study of cosmic radiation" and "communications in outer space." The 200 pupils, ranging from 14 to 17 years of age, traveled from as far away as Florida, California, New Mexico and the State of Washington to take the intensive four-week course.

In Oklahoma, the Frontiers of Science Foundation stimulates and supports summer education in mathematics and science. The Roscoe B. Jackson Memorial Laboratory at Bar Harbor, Maine, conducts summer programs for college students, pre-college students and biology teachers in which brilliant young minds are stimulated in basic research projects.

Industry participates extensively in summer science programs. The General Electric Foundation selected outstanding high school juniors to spend six weeks during a recent summer at Union College, in Schenectady, New York, engaging in pure research with the advice of any of the 400 staff scientists at the GE Research Laboratory they chose. There were no lectures, no classes, no formal instruction, no grades and no definite assignments. A total of 1,500 students sent inquiries about the program and 800 applied. A mere twenty were chosen.

Members of the Young Presidents Organization offer industrial opportunities also. In the spring of 1959, the YPO began summer internship programs to give students a chance to work closely with company presidents and other key officers. Each students is given an assignment that enables him to observe operations and, at the same time, fill a job for twelve weeks or so. At the end of his internship the student is required to submit a report on his observations of the company operations and an analysis of the strengths and weaknesses he has noted. Frankness is encouraged, with the result that management often learns something. One student developed a system for improving long-range financial forecasts for the Masury-Young Company of Boston. Roger Sonnabend reported that a teen-ager had designed and installed a control system for supplies at the Charterhouse Motor Hotel Division of the Hotel Corporation of America. A student devised an inexpensive anemometer to measure wind speeds at small airports for HRB-Singer, Inc. Two students who spent ten summer weeks at the company used an electronic computer to solve complicated problems that had stood in the way of perfecting a radar device and to develop a relatively inexpensive electronic warning system for alerting volunteer firemen in small communities.

Eight industrial concerns provided staff members for another voluntary science program, with no tests and no grades, for twenty-five selected students at the Glen Rock, New Jersey, High School. The companies admitted students to their laboratory facilities during the five-week course.

Always the numbers are limited. Horace Mann School, in New York, carefully selects a relatively few boys for an eight-week summer science program. A brain-twisting course for thirty top sophomore science students is conducted by the Delaware Summer Science Day Camp. Gifted Santa Barbara, California, youngsters study every morning for six weeks at a summer mathematics-science seminar and devote their afternoons to such complicated subjects as "probability and statistics," "organization and presentation of data—frequency distributions," "summarizing a set of measurements" and "an intuitive introduction to probability."

In at least one instance, a summer activity has proved so stimulating that it has given rise to a year-round educational experience. The Interlochen Music and Arts Camp in Michigan has been expanded into a twelve-month operation with the development of a Music and Arts Academy for gifted high school students. Dr. Joseph Maddy, founder of the camp, announced in the fall of 1961 plans to open a college preparatory boarding school in September, 1962, and the curriculum he organized called for 8 A.M. to 8 P.M. school work five days a week and *no* weekends off.

"When I started the camp," Maddy said, "the kids wanted to play music all summer. I found a place. Now they demand to do it all year around, and I intend to see that they do it. Our motto is 'learn more in less time' and we mean business."

This program is designed for the gifted youngster, but most offerings for the average yet interested students are severely limited. If a youngster is dull-witted or brilliant, he is welcome in special programs or summer schools, but most summer institutions do not have room for the in-between, nor will they have until year-round education is available—if it ever becomes available. There is a question whether all children should go to school around the year. The brilliant can be challenged by courses aimed at their intellectual level, particularly if the subjects are not regularly offered during the academic year. The slow pupils can be helped by remedial courses tailored to their capacity. But the middling students are better off, perhaps, doing something else with their summers. They probably can benefit more from camping, jobs, social service or any of the other constructive things to do in summer than from seeking out the classroom.

There is one upbeat summer experience for young people of almost any learning level, but it requires money and in rather impressive amounts. This is summer travel—with an emphasis on education rather than pleasure. A number of interesting itineraries are offered every summer for serious young travelers. One group of carefully selected members of high school student councils and their faculty advisers spent nearly seven weeks on an "international understanding" tour of Europe sponsored by the National Education Association. They called themselves "junior ambassadors," and each returned home to evaluate his experience carefully and plan ways to improve international relations through study, fund raising, peace rallies and the like.

Seminars and summer schools abroad are being organized to mix travel and study. Nearly 100,000 student passports were issued or renewed in 1960, marking an increase of 27 per cent over 1959.

Several colleges and universities sponsor summers abroad, among them Sarah Lawrence College and Fairleigh Dickinson University, both of which hold sessions near Florence. Travel agents organize small itinerant seminars that move from one university to another. Many students make their educational journeys alone, of course.

The National Student Association, representing 1,000,000 students in 400 United States colleges and universities, has a subsidiary called Educational Travel, Incorporated, which plans tours during which American students meet European students or engage in travel-study programs. In one program, a group studying French receives daily language lessons from Sorbonne professors and hears lectures by French instructors before breaking up for individual week-long visits with French families. Politics and economics are stressed on a Latin American tour. The most extensive program, a seventy-day, $1,000 tour of Eastern and Western Europe to make a comparative study of social institutions, offered three hours of academic credit.

Student exchanges are another important phase of educational travel. Foreign students come to America for year-long study while American students more often go abroad for only a summer to live with European families under a program financed by the American Field Service, which began as a World War I volunteer ambulance service and now is devoted almost entirely to youth work.

The YMCA and YWCA foster other programs, among them a U.S.A.-U.S.S.R. student exchange in which Americans go to the Soviet Union for a summer of travel and study and Russians are invited to pay similar visits to the United States.

Summer is a busy season for young people who want to work, serve or learn. The youngster with financial means to participate in study-travel programs is as rare as the gifted child to whom most of the summer enrichment courses are offered by schools. Some complaints have been registered because summer schools offer subjects not taught in the regular school year. Critics think there should be continuity between what preceded and what is to follow. Were this arranged, many of the gifted pupils seeking the stimulation offered by subjects both difficult and new to them might not be so interested in pursuing courses in the summer. Perhaps the reverse should prevail: the challenges of summer school might well be carried into the regular school year, particularly in view of the fact that summer instruction often is better than average.

As for service, so far the churches and related organizations have carried the major part of this load every summer. What they have done is slight, considering the number of young people available for such activity, but it is enormous considering the scope of the programs. Children need more than two weeks at camp or a weekly Scout meeting. Civic planners would be doing their communities a huge favor by tapping this reservoir of energy and ability—until such time as there are enough summer jobs for teen-agers who want them and more summer opportunities are offered by schools.

.14.

Camping With a Purpose

Early every summer, on the same day and at almost the same hour, thousands of children, some eager, some reluctant, are escorted by parents into the cavernous main waiting room of New York's Grand Central Terminal. Laden with duffle bags, knapsacks, air mattresses, suitcases and satchels, the youngsters gather around signs, most of them bearing Indian names, turn a sea of faces upward for farewell kisses and board trains.

This ritual, known as Leaving for Summer Camp, more or less marks the official opening of summer outdoor activities across the country for old and young. Camping has become so popular that some areas are running out of space in which to pitch tents and build campfires. Family camping, in which parents and children travel together, is growing in importance. Institutional camping, for families or for children, is still the most popular, but other camping activities are growing, among them work camps and caravans for older youth and educational camps for the gifted. Camping with a purpose is gaining ground on camping just for fun.

There are nearly 15,000 summer camps, with a total attendance of around 6,000,000. The American Recreation Association estimates that the number of child campers has increased in recent years at a faster rate than the total number of children—one of the few activities that has kept ahead of the population explosion. Children flock to camps conducted by long-established

147

organizations such as the Boy and Girl Scouts, Camp Fire Girls, YMCA, YWCA, YMHA, Community Chests, church groups and fraternal organizations, to name a few. They also attend privately owned commercial camps, many of them appealing to special interests.

Today's young people have a broad choice of the kind of camp they wish to attend. When organized camping was introduced in the United States more than a hundred years ago, however, recreation and physical fitness were stressed. With few exceptions, this was true until the mid-1930's, when "progressive educators" led the way in recognizing the special interests of unusual children and the abhorrence of some youngsters for organized physical exercise. Adults have begun to accept the fact that many children go along with the crowd in group sports when they would rather be reading, walking or doing almost anything else. For these individualistic children, summer camp used to be a shattering experience. Possibly it still is for some, but more are getting a chance to camp with a purpose, which for them is a far more stimulating experience than learning how to build a fire by rubbing two sticks together. Most organized institutional camps have little to offer the gifted child, and he has little to bring them. Older children, gifted and average, also balk at the traditional camp, partly because it no longer stimulates them and partly because they would prefer coeducational recreation.

For these and other reasons, a teen-ager sent to camp nowadays is likely to tuck ballet slippers or a slide rule into a knapsack along with a jackknife and a swimsuit. Standard camping gear often includes a violin or an oboe, sculpting tools, typewriters, textbooks or test tubes. In cramming a maximum of knowledge into the limited number of years allotted to growing up, bright youngsters do not want to waste a minute. Their haste to learn is involving them increasingly in being full-time students, which includes camping with a purpose.

The number and size of camps dedicated to the study of science, the arts, conservation and even college preparatory subjects have been growing steadily. They attract children who want to catch up on subjects in which they are weak or to develop abilities not sufficiently exploited in public schools. Many a parent is helping a child explore career possibilites by sending him to a specialized camp to find out if this area warrants further pursuit on a year-round basis. A boy, for example, may seem to lean toward a scientific interest; he can find out if this is a real bent during a summer of mathematics and chemistry at a laboratory-camp.

Youngsters who camp with a purpose work hard, but they also play. The principal reason they are at camp is to put their summer to good use, and this includes physical as well as mental exercise. But the athletic aspect of this kind of camping is no more important than the gymnasium period in school; it is just one activity, not *the* activity. The child who attends an educational camp may find more fun in learning than in doing anything else. Education is an adventure and camping can make it even more exciting. Serious summer campers appear to thrive on tough schedules such as that at one music camp, where a typical day involves taking lessons all morning, practicing in the afternoon and participating in recitals at night. Three hours of fun and games are tucked into each daily schedule, with a minimum of complaints from the campers.

Such establishments often are not camps in the traditional sense of occupying remote sites equipped with tents or cabins. Several universities offer dormitory and classroom facilities in the summer for "camps" in science or the performing arts. Utah State University, for one, sponsors a performing-arts summer workshop, with boys and girls living on the campus for five weeks of work and study in dance, drama and music before touring national parks for three weeks. College or high school credit is given for attendance.

The Girls Friendly Society of the Protestant Episcopal Church conducts a "camp" in a St. Louis mansion, where girls develop their talents in the fine and performing arts. An estate built by the late J. P. Morgan is the home of the Fokine Ballet Camp, which boasts a large swimming pool and tennis court as well as a dance studio on its twelve acres. Girls study ballet for eight weeks within walking distance of the Tanglewood Music Festival. "Field trips" are made to concerts, summer plays and Jacob's Pillow dance performances, and boys from neighboring camps are invited to weekly parties. Mayfair Hall, at Hunter, New York, specializes in the theater arts, providing instruction in acting, directing, writing and the application of stage make-up. Camp Tanglewood, in the Berkshires, teaches music appreciation on field trips to summer music festivals in the area. The Pickwick School conducts an experimental program for forty New England teen-age boys and girls who plan and construct buildings and engage in related projects such as landscaping, interior decorating and tending forests.

There are hundreds of these camps, each offering something a youngster can take home with him beside dried leaves and wood carvings. Learning to drive an automobile is one of the subjects taught at Lincoln Farm, in Roscoe, New York, which is for "alert teen-agers who have outgrown conventional camps." Preparation for a "teen-agers' foreign exchange program" is offered at the International Camp in the Berkshires, where youngsters study foreign languages. Camp Saskatchewan, in Adirondack, New York, teaches typing, languages, journalism and the arts, which are hardly subjects the originators of outdoorsmanship for children had in mind with the pioneering summer camps. Six weeks of study in mathematics, biology, geology, chemistry, physics, meteorology and astronomy are offered to boys from 12 to 15 years of age at the Adirondack Science Camp at Plattsburgh, New York.

Music is a favorite subject at camps extending from Arrowbear Lake Music Camp, in California, where 100 boys and girls play in a summer orchestra under the trees and stars, to the Transylvania Music Camp in Brevard, North Carolina, where 210 youngsters, their hi-fis far behind them, play long-hair music and sing in a chorus.

Camps devoted to science are becoming more numerous as juvenile interest in the subject increases. One of the more successful establishments is Rancho Sawatch, in Buena Vista, Colorado, where boys are taught conservation, wildlife management, entomology, geology, mineralogy and forestry and then practice what they have learned on two-week camping field trips. This sort of mixture of old-fashioned and new-fashioned camping has attracted many youngsters.

Accompanying the specialized camp have been such opportunities as travel camps, day camps near home and urban summer activities that are labeled simply "outdoor education." The sightseeing camping trips may involve a few youngsters being driven in a station wagon or a band of chattering girls touring the Canadian Rockies in a private Pullman car. One travel camp is an annual escorted tour of Mexico for the study of the native arts. Another is a summer safari through the Black Hills of South Dakota and other Western national parks. These trips often are comparatively expensive, although not so costly as European camping trips, where a ten-week journey may come to at least $1,500.

An example of the successful nomadic adventure is Camp Cheechako, which has all North America for its campsite. Organized by the YMCA in Keene, New Hampshire, Cheechako conducts trips during school vacations all year 'round. In the first years after it was founded in 1959, Cheechako took its campers on visits to twenty-three states and Canada. Youngsters from 11 to 17 years of age and in groups ranging from six to forty climbed mountains, skied, went deep-sea fishing and visited industrial plants, rodeos and historical sites on trips carefully planned months in advance. For the summer of 1962 the campers mapped a seven-week trip to Alaska, planned so well that they had listed all the points of interest along the route and the costs of meals and campsites at every stop.

Such programs are growing, but no outdoor recreational activities have expanded as have those of religious organizations. The growth of religion-oriented camps has outstripped that of all other types combined. Some of the earliest outdoor recreational facilities in the country were "Bible camps" serving large groups, often hundreds at a time. The trend in church camping now is toward decentralization, with groups often limited to fifty or sixty. Local churches increasingly are sponsoring their own camps, rather than joining with other groups, so they can continue their programs without interruption. Church-sponsored family camps and conferences are another recent development. Leaders say that the idea that summer belongs to children alone no longer is accepted.

Families are joining children in the outdoors for many reasons, the main one possibly being that they are scurrying back to nature to escape some of the pressures of modern life. Refugees from crowded cities, fugitives from the high cost of traveling and escapists from world tensions have joined in making family camping a major activity. Highways hum with automobiles crammed with camping gear or pulling trailers. Campers go deluxe, with mattresses and refrigerators in house trailers, or rough it without even so much as a pup tent over their heads. There are wayside campsites for families who find tenting more economical and more fun than hotel or motel vacation stopovers, and there are city parks that provide sites made homey with television and plumbing.

Family touring and camping have become a major recreational interest now that fathers have longer vacations to spend with their children. Although it is the oldest form of camping, it is comparatively new to Americans, and its growth in the last few years has been so great that parks and forests have not been prepared for the rush. In the summer of 1960, for example, more than 40,000 family groups were turned away from crowded sites in the Michigan state parks. A shortage of camping spaces in Wisconsin state parks caused angry protests by taxpayers. California authorities found that there were only 55,000 public picnic sites in the state, whereas 150,000 would be needed by 1980.

National parks and forests are jammed in the summer, often raising the question of why some of the would-be campers left home in the first place; it might have been less congested where they were. Commercial campsites are being expanded, but national and state parks have been slow to catch on to the interest in camping and they are the places most frequently sought by travelers who like to live outdoors as inexpensively as possible.

Campfires are glowing across America, even in the nation's capital. To ease the demand for tourist accommodations—and to fill the desire to camp—a tentsite has been established only a few minutes' drive from the White House. The Potomac Park Motor Court, with tent areas and spaces for trailers, is part of the Capital Park System. So heavy is the demand for space that stays are limited to two weeks. The success of this pioneering establishment indicates a need for similar sites in or near other major cities drawing large numbers of tourists.

The interest in family camping has become so great that recreation experts are conducting training courses for greenhorns. In Washington, D.C., the American Camping Association and the YMCA have a family camping workshop. Several colleges and universities offer special courses in outdoor living techniques, and the New Hampshire Recreation Society sponsors an annual Family Camporee to help families make the transition from city living. The first things the "students" learn are how to pitch a tent and build a campfire.

Recreationists are turning their attention also to the stay-at-homes, mainly children, who either do not wish to camp or do not have money for it. There are many charitable camps for the destitute, underprivileged or physically handicapped, but it is doubtful that there is a charitable camp for gifted children. Some specialized camps offer a limited number of scholarships to those who are deserving and cannot afford tuition of $500 to $600 for eight weeks away from home. For the rest, outdoor education programs in camplike settings are the only answer. Here the growth has been slow in the twenty years since such activities were introduced. There are between 500 and 600 local programs conducted by schools, many of them related to regular courses in science, conservation, history, geography and physical education. To encourage such projects, the Carnegie Corporation has given $120,000 to Sciences and Arts Camps, Incorporated, which started with a single day camp in Darien, Connecticut, in 1960 and has been growing slowly since. Grade school children are offered courses in Russian, communications and philosophy in addition to art and music, and they meet on weekends for refresher discussions during the academic year.

Other day camps offer a taste of what it is like to live "next to nature." The Minneapolis Park Board has established such a program on the edge of the city, in a forest where children visit a park museum and hike along a trail. They see the largest tree in Minneapolis and the nest of a hawk. After swimming and fishing in a pond, the youngsters cook supper over fires and then board buses for home.

The Audubon Park Day Camp in Memphis, Tennessee, is similar. Some overnight trips are offered by the Moosejaw Day Camp in Colorado Springs, which teaches children to read compasses and hunt fossils.

These programs are for younger children. For older ones there is still another kind of camping, which has attracted considerable interest. It is the volunteer work camp, born during the reconstruction of Europe after World War I and brought to the United States by the American Society of Friends, which opened its first camp near Greensburg, Pennsylvania, in 1934. A number of religious and community organizations now sponsor work camps that offer hard labor and few, if any, of the conventional outdoor activities of the traditional camps. Private work camps are less rigorous, usually having schedules calling for half a day of work and half a day of conventional camping lore.

Character building and experience in cooperative living are the chief by-products of full-time voluntary work camps, where life is simple and the participants learn a degree of self-discipline as well as how to get along with all kinds of people. While they are at it, they make themselves useful. These camps bring together youngsters from varying religious, racial, economic, educational and geographic backgrounds. The campers pay at least part of their own expenses in order to work harder than they ever have before. One of these "camps" actually is in a Harlem, New York City, tenement, with the "campers" engaged in repairing surrounding buildings. Another has been held in a St. Louis slum. During a recent summer, medical students gathered in Oakland, California, to work days in full-time jobs and devote their spare time to trying to relate Christianity to their profession. This also was called camping.

The American Friends Service Committee program, prototype of the others, accepts campers from nineteen to thirty years of age, with twenty to thirty persons of all nationalities and races in each camp. A typical program calls for an average of thirty-six hours of manual work a week for seven weeks, daily worship, Bible study, discussion of current events and recreation. One American Friends camp was installed at a mental hospital, where campers worked with patients. Another made a survey of attitudes toward minority groups in Bucks County, Pennsylvania.

Annual projects for senior high school students and older youth are sponsored by The Methodist Church. Groups worked one summer among the Houma Indians at the Dulac, Louisiana, Indian Center, at an interracial camp near Nashville, Tennessee, and at a Blackfoot Indian Mission in Montana. There have been camps to construct facilities for Negro schools and provide recreation for underprivileged children in cities. Young people pay token fees for the opportunity of doing nearly all such work.

The Methodist Youth Department turned down as many youngsters as were accepted in 1961, a record year, and applications continued to flow in even after the campers had set to work. A search for adventure sometimes is as much a motive as a desire to be useful, and in a preponderance of cases the young campers acknowledge that they probably would have to stay at home for the summer if it was not for the work camps. One questions the use of the word "camp" to describe many of the programs, particularly a "work camp" in the vacation paradise of Honolulu, where Luther Leaguers, at a cost of $350 each, helped maintain buildings and yards at St. Paul's Church and assisted in its vacation Bible school.

Hard work is the only guarantee offered by the American Jewish Society for Service at its annual interdenominational summer work service camps. Youngsters pay up to $175 to work for seven weeks at such tasks as building homes in a slum area of Indianapolis or constructing a barn and maintaining buildings and grounds at a welfare camp in Illinois.

Paralleling such programs are work caravans, started in 1948 by the Congregational Christian Churches to provide young people with a better understanding of the church's youth work and to give them something to do in the summer. Since their formation the caravans have covered considerable ground, repairing and building church facilities, working on school and camp buildings and doing any other chores they are assigned. All the work has some social significance—so much, in fact, that a number of boys have decided to enter the ministry as a result of their summer experiences.

Other church groups have organized caravans for older teen-agers. Record numbers applied for acceptance in 1961, so many that even well-qualified youngsters had to be rejected. Caravan organizers found that for the first time they were rejecting boys. Usually more girls than boys have applied and been accepted, but in 1961 the teams were evenly divided. The boy who participated had applied even before the 1961 scarcity of summer jobs became apparent.

Caravanning, too, is regarded as camping, although in many cases the worker-travelers stay in dormitories or parsonages as they make their rounds. The groups, always chaperoned, occasionally camp while en route, but this is not often the case.

All the recreational activities, whether a day in a park, eight weeks of outdoor study or a month of hard labor, are welcomed warmly by officials from the White House to the smallest hamlet. There has been considerable talk about a recreational crisis in the United States and much complaining that the space allotted for playgrounds of all types is not being expanded rapidly enough to meet the growing population. Cities large and small are trying to develop parksites before they are clogged with buildings, and the Federal Government should be doing so, too. There is a great need for more facilities for family camping and for camps for youngsters who want summer to be a challenge.

.15.

For God and Country

THE NATION'S YOUTH HAD A READY ANSWER WHEN THE YOUNG President pleaded in his inaugural address, "Do not ask what your country can do for you, but what you can do for your country."

Their answer was to give themselves.

President Kennedy's Peace Corps, an added starter in the international race for friends in the Cold War, was greeted as a "pep pill" for young people, who heeded the summons with an enthusiasm that surprised some of the most optimistic of their elders. Young people have responded to calls for service to God and country without asking, "What are the hours?" "How much is the pay?" "When does the vacation begin" or "How about overtime?" Whether the Corps makes its mark or not, it will have achieved something by displacing the "ugly American" with youth, and by bringing public attention to the good works already being performed abroad, largely by church organizations.

Youth service had been glorified in war, but the Peace Corps changed all that. There were lampooners, to be sure, such as the columnist Robert Ruark, who could not resist the temptation to call the Corps "overgrown Boy Scouts" and the "Kiddie Korps," and the *Yale Daily News* editorial writer who said the Corps promised to be little more than a new "Children's Crusade." But this sort of comment never grew loud and soon died away.

When Kennedy announced his plan to dispatch tractor drivers, teachers and road builders to help underdeveloped countries, he reflected, although perhaps not consciously, the missionary zeal that had been burgeoning among American youth since World War II. The nation's religious upsurge had set off a post-war rush overseas to work on missionary projects. It probably was at least partly responsible for the enthusiastic response to the Presidential call mustering the Peace Corps.

An impressive number of the Corps' volunteers had been students at church-related colleges but did not want to become missionaries. Some of the larger Protestant denominations and the Roman Catholic Church welcomed the Corps and urged their own young people to apply.

Volunteers accepted by the Peace Corps receive subsistence allowances plus $75 a month, which is accumulated as separation pay so they will have something to live on until they find jobs after their two-year tours of duty are over.

There is a considerable degree of interest in service on the part of young people. They have seen how the Good Neighbor Policy, the Point Four Program for Technical Assistance to Underdeveloped Countries and the Marshall Plan dramatized ways for one group to help others. The "sit-in" and "freedom ride" demonstrations in the segregated South whetted their interest in getting into areas of controversy. There surely also must be a connection between their desire for service and their worry over the complex world situation. They know that they cannot deal with the problem individually, so they want to participate in some small way in the search for a solution. It consoles them to know that they are at least *trying* to help.

Then, too, there is a "back-to-nature" philosophy in the approach of many young persons. They feel they have been living in a civilization that has been getting too soft and rich.

"I find life too easy here," said Gordon Culp, who at 23 was one of the first Peace Corps volunteers. Culp, then a student at Stevens Institute of Technology in Hoboken, New Jersey, said there was nothing he wanted to do more than use his technical knowledge in underdeveloped countries, and the Peace Corps would give him this chance. He asked for duty as near the Equator as possible, explaining that he liked a hot climate. When he left home at 17, he headed straight for a steaming Mexican jungle, where he collected moths and butterflies and ate rattlesnake meat. He then joined a trailer-ferry company and went to Havana, and, at 20, he invented a machine to unload large sugar cargoes from ships.

"The machine can have important applications in the growing of food," Culp said. "Actually, it is the growth of food in underdeveloped countries which interests me now."

Matthew DeForest, a 31-year-old Chicago truck driver with a high school education, scored near the top in the first Peace Corps qualification tests. He is skilled at handling bulldozers and machines and speaks fluent Spanish. Asked why he signed up, he replied:

"This may sound corny, but I think our first duty is toward God, then toward our country and then toward ourselves. I think the Peace Corps is good because it can help us serve all three.

"We need to retell our story in this world. We have to communicate somehow with the people in other countries. We have to show them what Americans are really like. And the only way to do that is to have Americans go to those countries and show them."

Then there was Mike Lanigan, 23, of Falls Church, Virginia, former Marine, son of a Marine Corps general and a handyman by inclination. "It'll be a good feeling," he said, "to pack up and go somewhere to do something worthwhile."

Among the early assignments of Peace Corpsmen were the improvement of poultry and swine culture and development of irrigation systems on the West Indies island of Santa Lucia; a road survey in Tanganyika, in East Africa; a rural development program in Colombia, and the introduction of elementary science and English in schools in the Philippines.

The projects had a familiar ring to many organizations that have been active abroad, but especially to the church groups. The only really new thing they could see about the Kennedy Corps was that it was government-financed and sponsored and seemed to be looking for Phi Beta Kappas who could drive tractors. The first commitments were about the same as those of missionaries, fraternal workers and ecumenical volunteers assigned by the churches to spread the Gospel in an era of international evangelism geared to the Cold War and the Atomic Age. It is an evangelism in which many missionaries cannot even call themselves by that name but must accept the label of fraternal worker instead. They are barred in many places from openly proselytizing for Christianity. They are welcome to perform good works but not to seek converts in other lands, most notably India.

Regardless of how much he knows about the United States Constitution and its Bill of Rights and how much he wants to talk about them, the Peace Corps volunteer also is barred from proselytizing. It is his job to work and live among the nationals of the country to which he is sent and to hope he makes friends for America. But a word of praise of the way of life back home in Indiana is likely to result in a one-way ticket to the banks of the Wabash.

Wherever Peace Corpsmen go, they almost invariably find the churches were there first. The schools in which they teach most likely were church-financed; some still are, the others having been turned over to host governments. The hospitals where corpsmen work are for the most part mission installations. Many of the doctors are medical missionaries.

It took 250 years for the churches to open the way now being taken by the Peace Corps. The first Protestant missionaries went out to India from Europe in 1706, but the great modern outpouring of witnesses from the English-speaking churches did not begin until 1793. There was a sacrificial air about the departures of the first young American missionaries, from Salem and Boston, Massachusetts, in the early Nineteenth Century, for they had no expectation of returning home. In those days, in which there were no furloughs, social security or pension plans, it took so long to reach a station that a missionary remained there until he died.

These early missionaries had but one goal, to establish Christianity around the globe. Afterwards, the missionary became a specialist—a doctor, teacher, nurse, geologist, engineer or technician. The first technical-assistance programs were carried out 150 years ago by medical evangelists. Now mission work often is little different from that of the civilian Peace Corps.

Independent "peace corps" have been formed by several church organizations. The Lutherans recruited hundreds of professional men and women, skilled workers and students to serve as part-time missionaries entirely at their own expense. Fourteen dentists in Minneapolis and St. Paul volunteered to serve three months every two years in mission clinics or dispensaries. Students enrolled in universities abroad to form "Christian cells" to counteract anti-Christian propaganda. The United Presbyterian Church in the U.S.A. had its own peace corps, too, and the United Church of Christ and The Methodist Church have special-term missionaries, who, like Peace Corpsmen, serve overseas on three-year tours of duty.

YMCA Junior World Service secretaries work for a year or two at nominal pay building camps overseas. It took the "Y" a century to build its global service program. In some cases, a junior secretary is given as much as two years of training before being dispatched to a hardship area.

"You can't just take a kid out of college and send him to the Congo," a "Y" official said.

The service organization has sent technicians to Mexico to teach new farming techniques—but by "new" they do not mean the latest. They regard a program based on advanced methods as being as ridiculous as it would be to try to teach an African to use a flush toilet when he does not know how to dig a latrine.

The Mexicans are shown how to use earthworms, plentiful there, to enrich the soil. If a crooked stick is all they have ever had for tilling the soil, a hoe is a giant step forward.

So many organizations are involved in socio-religious activity abroad that Protestant groups have formulated extensive co-operative programs in which representatives of several denominations work in the same mission facility. In line with this interdenominational effort to eliminate duplications costly in money and precious manpower, some church leaders believe that the Peace Corps and similar groups sent out by other countries should be a United Nations endeavor. This, of course, would result in the United States' paying most of the bills but being barred from taking any credit. What President Kennedy had in mind with his Peace Corps undoubtedly was the formation of an all-American task force to establish beachheads for democracy in countries that are targets of Communist propagandists.

Just as the missionary is a "diplomat without portfolio," so the Peace Corpsman is expected to serve as an agent of the government. The number of corpsmen in the field is bound to be skimpy during the first experimental years. However, there are 35,000 American Protestant and Catholic missionaries in service abroad, and they represent their country as well as their churches.

Some of the more experienced denominations have given much help and advice to the Peace Corps. One Protestant leader said that R. Sargent Shriver, director of the Corps, and his aides "picked our brains" to find out in a few weeks what the churches had spent generations learning. The churchmen were glad to help because, as one of them said, whether they actively participate in the Peace Corps program, they are a part of it simply because their efforts are similar. There is a tendency on the part of churchmen to take a "show me" attitude toward the Peace Corps, which some regard as an "interloper" or "upstart," and they seldom fail to comment that "we were there first."

Three types of Peace Corps projects were set up—those run

entirely by the government, those let out on contract to organizations and those already in progress under independent auspices but adaptable to the Peace Corps program. CARE, the food-parcel distributing organization, signed an early agreement, for work in Colombia. Notre Dame University signed another. The Heifer Project, a farming service, and Crossroads Africa, which recruits students to do manual labor in Africa, also took assignments. Roman Catholic groups warmly welcomed the prospect of participation, despite Shriver's insistence that all units must include persons of all religions. The Catholics said they would be glad to accept members of other faiths on their teams but reserved the right to reject persons of no faith or belief.

Some Protestant organizations balked at contractual relationships with the government but at the same time declared their support of the Corps and its objectives. The question of separation of church and state was raised, but more serious was the matter of being required to represent the nation always, but the church never. Dr. Earl S. Erb, executive secretary of the Board of Foreign Missions of the United Lutheran Church in America, said that the Corps was contrary to all the church stood for and that the church's primary mission was to proclaim the Gospel, not to assume "institutional responsibilities." The United Presbyterian Church in the U.S.A. ruled out contracts with the Corps but offered its resources for training and orienting corpsmen. The Presbyterians told Shriver the Corps should not have church groups in its employ, and the American Jewish Congress took a similar stand, pleading separation of church and state and also suggesting that the Corps might be handicapped by the inclusion of church groups.

Shriver was frank in stating that the Peace Corps wanted to capitalize on the experience of church welfare agencies overseas, but that at the same time they could not proselytize once they joined forces with his battalions. The churches felt, and rightly so, that they would not be performing their duty were

they to stop reading the Sermon on the Mount and take as
their text the Declaration of Independence.

The Peace Corps, born in a campaign promise, is in itself
promising despite some of the obstacles encountered in its
formative months. Congress enacted legislation making it a
permanent government agency, on a people-to-people level, but
to fight problems, not other people. Recruits are going out to
do tasks outlined by host countries in the economic, social and
educational fields and to establish personal relationships of their
own creation. The men and women in charge of the Peace
Corps know that they are combating a formidable Cold War foe
in those who are working arduously as missionaries for Communism in the underdeveloped countries. But they hope that
the presence of unbrainwashed Americans, most of them fresh-
faced young people, will counteract the Communist pressure.
This hope may be naïve, but, nevertheless, the Peace Corps may
at last answer the call, made more than half a century ago by the
philosopher William James, for the development of a "moral
equivalent of war."

.16.

Young Men in a Hurry

THE SONS OF THE "LOST GENERATION" HAVE BECOME LEADERS of business and industry. At the end of World War II, they were serious young veterans in too much of a hurry to heed the laments of tired old titans that high taxes, paternalistic government and demanding labor unions had taken the incentive out of getting rich. While many of the elders grumbled, the new generation went to work to prove that it still was possible to build a fortune with grit and a willingness to gamble.

There are success stories galore about young tycoons, whether they are "egghead" millionaires who drive old cars and wear rumpled suits or rich young men who have become richer. A remarkable number of fortunes have been built without the benefit of college degrees—some even without high school educations. Almost every young tycoon has displayed at least a trace of daring and quite a bit of ingenuity, keeping sharp eyes out for new developments and the changing tastes of consumers. The space age has provided a whole new area for fortune building, as have the housing boom, the sports car fad and the development of coin-operated laundries. Door-to-door selling, one of the oldest businesses in the world, has seen a rapid expansion since World War II, and it has been the young men not the veterans in the field, who have supervised the growth.

Many of the new millionaires are loners; they may have been Boy Scouts but they are not organization men. Others are more gregarious, but the groups they seek out are interested in society, not socializing; they want organizations for men, not overgrown Boy Scouts.

This new philosophy is best expressed perhaps by the Young Presidents Organization, a creature of the post-war generation, with membership open to anyone under 40 who heads a company employing at least fifty persons and reporting an annual gross income of $1,000,000 or more. In actuality, the 2,000 members average 39 years of age, 200 employees and annual sales of $3,500,000. At 40, a man is "too old" for membership and must "retire" from the club.

The Young Presidents Organization—known as YPO—was formed in 1950 by war veterans who had inherited their fathers' businesses, but soon the membership also included men with up-from-nothing success stories. Now the members are about evenly divided between those who took over from relatives or married the boss's daughter and those who made their own successes.

YPOers reflect a general trend toward younger executives. The post-war generation of business leaders generally is ten to twenty years younger than its pre-war predecessors. The new tycoons seem to be more progressive and better oriented to new methods. They try to make educated approaches to business practices, participating in seminars and courses on how to run a business and always looking for new production and management methods. Unlike some of the older men on the tycoon level, they are constantly thinking about giving chances to other young people in their own organizations.

The YPO sponsors nearly 200 business meetings a year for its members and potential members. In a new development— for businessmen, at least—wives are taken into both corporate confidences and YPO meeting rooms. These young men feel that their wives must give them strong support in the early days of sacrifice in building a business, and so they include women to an extent that the aging veteran of fun-and-games conventions must find astonishing.

YPO conducts an active campaign in schools through student panel discussions. Members contribute their time to this effort in the hope that they can stimulate students to want to be more than cogs in a business machine. The presidents feel that their time has been well invested if only a few students in each session "catch the torch of individual enterprise and progressive business philosophy."

A major effort is being made to reach students who will not go to college. It began with an economic workshop at Montclair State College, in New Jersey, to develop a curriculum for teaching high school commercial students how businesses are run. Information given teachers to take to their schools included such topics as trade unions and their "legitimate objectives," labor-management relations, international trade and pricing in a market economy. These were woven into the teaching of typing, bookkeeping and other office subjects, and were included in a textbook prepared by YPOers and the teachers who took the course.

YPO research shows that men reach presidential rank in the largest American companies at an average age of about 52. Members of YPO, whose enterprises are more modest in size, make it twenty years earlier. A president at 52 holds his job for an average of seven years. The young president figures on staying put for an average of twenty-six years before retiring. His annual salary may be lower, but his long-range earning outlook is much better. The presidents of the 500 largest corporations average a little less than $75,000 a year. Nearly a third of the Young Presidents are doing that well now.

The self-made tycoon reaches his peak position a little later but works harder and is more dynamic than the president of a family-controlled business. Strong feelings of civic responsibility are almost universal among the young presidents. They average three outside activities a year, giving about 10 per cent of their working hours to community and public work, as an expression of the philosophy of their organization, which is:

"After you have achieved success at corporate homemaking, it is time to take another bride. . . . It's time to turn your talents to the good of the community that helped build you. . . . If you are the busiest man in town, that is all the more reason . . . for the busier you are, the more you can do."

The very existence of the Young Presidents Organization is an indication of the extent of the activity of youth in the world of commerce. There is as much interest in wanting to be helpful in the area of awesome international problems as in trying to take the "bugs" out of a production line. Members of YPO feel there is a general lack of understanding of what Communism is all about, so they study subjects in the socio-economic sphere that old-line chiefs of industry must find puzzling.

In other respects, too, the new tycoon is a different breed. Many of the young presidents of rapidly growing companies live far more modestly than necessary because they are putting profits back into their businesses. The older executive may tend to make all he can while he can; the younger one looks further ahead. YPOers are interested in the long-range future of the economy and the country and therefore work for the future. They find that it is difficult to talk to a 60-year-old man today about problems that may develop twenty years from now. A younger man with an actuarial chance of being around in the 1980's can contemplate the future more realistically—and therefore more enthusiastically.

The Young Presidents represent every form of business, with manufacturing making up slightly more than half the membership. Ten per cent of the men head two companies. Nearly all are married. They have an average of 3.4 children. Ninety-four per cent attended college, 72 per cent graduated and 60 per cent did post-graduate work.

One of the self-made young presidents is Edward A. White, son of an electrician, a ham radio operator at 13 and a teen-age laboratory research worker at Harvard during the war. By the time he was 33, he had been head of the Bowmar Instrument

Corporation, a Fort Wayne manufacturer of tiny missile parts, for several years and sales had reached about $4,000,000 a year.

After leaving his job at Harvard, White studied electrical engineering at Tufts and then joined the Capehart-Farnsworth Corporation as a junior engineer at the advanced age of 19. He began hearing talk of a need for tiny mechanisms for huge missiles and jet aircraft. This was all he needed to quit his job and, with his modest savings, set up shop in a two-car garage, where he developed high-speed precision counters and gearheads.

With his wife, Joan, keeping the books, White achieved sales of $55,000 the first year and $238,000 the second. In 1955, he turned out a counter only a quarter-inch in diameter for a Polaris atomic submarine's control panel. He hired more help until his work force had reached 400 and he had built a plant many times larger than a two-car garage.

Roland Bixler, president of J-B-T Instrument, Incorporated, of New Haven, Connecticut, manufacturer of instruments and electrical components, is typical of the public-spirited "new" executive. Bixler is chairman of the board of New Haven College and a member of the Woodridge, Connecticut, board of education. He is a trustee of his alma mater, Bluffton College, in Ohio, and was a delegate to the White House Conference on Education. As a father of two children, he served as chairman of his local Parent-Teachers Association and helped launch an annual town business-industry-education day during which teachers tour plants and offices to observe the parents of their pupils at work.

"The very nature of any president's job," says Bixler, "requires that he look ahead, not only to plan for the future of his respective business, but also to do everything possible to insure a healthy future climate for his children. He naturally must be concerned about the economic, social and political atmosphere which best assures opportunities for all Americans. In that context, what can be more important than developing our future human resources through education?"

Bill Eberle, president of a car rental agency and a large

laundry and dry cleaning business in Idaho, represents the politically minded new millionaire. Eberle became so disturbed by the absence of young business people in rank-and-file government and political party posts that he decided to act. He ran for state Representative, but lost by 100 votes. Then he went to work as a salesman—selling his party on business men in politics. He began at the bottom, by winning election as a precinct committeeman. His next step was to persuade other young people in business to take part in party precinct activities. Soon teams of business people were in action; they waged a campaign so successful that it sent Eberle to the State House with a large majority. He was re-elected as a representative twice, serving as majority leader in one term and minority leader in another, and he also was state finance chairman of his party.

In the Legislature, Eberle was instrumental in winning revision of the state law on youth and delinquency, and in overhauling the state income and business tax laws, in developing a mental-health program and in improving the schools.

"The time taken for the Legislature is well rewarding," he says, "not financially, but in terms of accomplishments for the public good."

Eberle and other outstanding YPOers have followed the organization's four-point formula for success:

1. Teach yourself organization and self-discipline at the beginning of your business life, whether you become president or not.
2. Gear this pattern into every waking hour: "The more you do . . . the more you can do."
3. Put this pattern to work by applying your talents to helping others with the same vigor that you have applied to build your business.
4. Once a civic problem has been solved, look for a bigger one —"you're only as big as the problem with which you're dealing."

"It is quite obvious that these young presidents are driven by a fuel-injection system far hotter than that of the average businessman," says a YPO official, "but then, could they have reached the presidency while still so young without it?"

The answer lies not only in a study of members of the YPO organization but of the nonorganization men who have made successes. There is no tabulation of the tycoons and otherwise successful young citizens who are not members of any group, but it is certain that there are many. Some are so quiet and modest about their work that only those close to them have any idea how rich and powerful they may be.

There is no doubt in financial circles that more persons have built large fortunes in the era of "high taxes and no incentive" than in the supposedly freer economic air of the 1920's. Inflation has reduced the value of a million dollars, but it still is a fortune.

If there are any success secrets harbored by the self-made successes, they surely must include a willingness to work hard and to risk failure. For every new millionaire there doubtless are many men who were financial flops. Perhaps a glance at some of the success stories will give a clue to some of the secrets.

Consider Harry S. Stonehill, for example. He was one of the veterans of World War II who did not come home, choosing instead to remain among the people he had helped to liberate—in this case, the Filipinos. Stonehill, born in St. Louis, reared in Chicago and educated in accounting at the University of Illinois, had only his Army discharge papers when he began his rapid rise to being a multi-millionaire in Manila. He began by selling war surplus through a trading company, but soon branched out into the import and sale of refrigerators. Innovations caused his business to prosper. First he advertised widely, something Filipinos had not yet learned to do; then he created a homey atmosphere in his display rooms, inviting housewives to sit down for a soft drink and a chat. He cut his prices and increased volume.

Once this business was on the way, so was Harry Stonehill, still in his 30's. He introduced Virginia tobacco and a cigarette factory to a previously impoverished area. Then came a window-glass manufacturing plant. Stonehill's enterprises launched a reclamation project to turn 7,300 acres of Manila Bay into a site for low-cost houses. They built the first such housing in Manila. Potentially the biggest success came to Stonehill when a crew he sent out with water-drilling equipment to study surface rock formations struck oil at a mere 240 feet. They were only scratching the surface when they made the important find.

What is success to Stonehill?

"It's always that little plus factor," he said. "It's the man who thinks about his business after 5 o'clock, who gets just a little bit ahead. Basically most of us are about the same intellectually from every respect. But you have to give a little extra thought on how to get ahead. In my case, it isn't a formula, but I have worked a little bit harder. I know that I'm not any brighter. An important thing is a friendly attitude—liking people and getting along with people."

James L. Ling of Dallas is another member of the young millionaires' club who started at the bottom. His original investment was $3,800. Thirteen years later, at the age of 38, his assets amounted to more than $10,000,000 and were rising.

Ling, who originally wanted to be a priest, ran away from home without graduating from high school. Yet he became president and chairman of the executive committee and biggest stockholder in Ling-Temco Electronics, Incorporated, with factories scattered across the country. His products include electronic vibration and accoustical testing equipment, radar devices for early-warning systems, sonar systems for submarine detection, closed-circuit television systems, vacuum tubes, hi-fi sets and satellite tracking devices. His sales in 1960 reached $150,000,000 and his income about $150,000.

At 19, Ling got a job with an electrical contractor and went to school to become an electrician. The Navy completed his education during World War II. After his discharge, he bought a truck and opened an electrical shop, slowly building business by borrowing money. When his business reached firm ground, he astounded financiers by selling $250,000 worth of stock after distributing prospectuses at a state fair.

Ling and his wife, Dorothy, a former secretary, live in an expensive home and drive costly automobiles but they have very little social life. Sundays are reserved for the children. Ling never has taken a vacation.

His success advice is to the point: You need education and you must learn to think. Examine both the negative and positive sides of every business proposition. Do not wait for business to come to you; go out and find the business. Work fast and be impatient.

Gordon O. Baskin saw opportunity in something new—automatic laundry appliances. As a result, he became one of the youngest bank presidents in the country. Baskin, married and the father of five, worked his way through UCLA selling hot dogs at football games, selling shoes and driving a taxi. After receiving a degree in economics and business administration, he opened a "model store" for washers and driers, using a bank loan of $2,000 to finance the operation. Three years later, after introducing new techniques that were copied in other similar stores, Baskin sold out for $25,000 and went into the real estate business. His biggest deal involved development of a million-dollar hotel on Hollywood's Sunset Strip. From there to banking was an easy step for Baskin, who in 1961 founded the Continental Bank in Los Angeles. The president is Gordon O. Baskin. The vice president and secretary is William C. Herron, the banker who gave Baskin his $2,000 loan.

John L. Russell found *his* fortune in one of the oldest "products" in the world—the Bible. At the age of 32, after wartime service and door-to-door selling for other companies, Russell founded his business, Advance Distributors, Incorporated, which specializes in the sale of family Bibles. From a total of 100 Bibles a week, the company has grown so rapidly that its annual gross now is around $7,000,000. Russell, a native of Bogalusa, Louisiana, tried both indoor and outdoor selling after he finished business college. He became convinced there was no future in working for someone else, so he settled for direct selling as a career. His decision to begin his own business came when the company he worked for stopped handling Protestant Bibles, Russell's "best-seller."

Ambition is Russell's explanation for his success. "Every year of my life," he says, "I was ambitious."

Hot-rodding made a millionaire of Robert Peterson, bachelor publisher of a hot-rod magazine, six automotive magazines and a periodical containing articles on teen-age entertainers, fashion tips and advice to teen-age girls on how to get along with parents and dates. Sales of this Los Angeles venture total about $10,-000,000 a year, and Peterson's personal fortune is estimated at $3,500,000.

The son of European immigrants, Peterson grew up in Barstow, California, where he worked first as a grocery clerk and then as a train crew roundup boy, a well driller's helper and a service station attendant. In the last job, he accepted used tires as payment for gasoline from jobless travelers en route to Los Angeles. Then he resold the tires, paid the station for the gasoline and kept the difference. After two semesters at Montana State College at the expense of the United States Army, Peterson turned movie press agent for $35 a week. He became involved in a hot-rod show that was so successful he decided to launch his first magazine.

Kjell H. Qvale owes his success to foreign sports cars and his early recognition that they were going to be popular in America. The teetotaling son of a Norwegian sea captain, Qvale came to the United States as a child, left the University of Washington to pilot naval transports in World War II and invested $10,000 saved from his flight pay to open an auto agency in Alameda, California. He began with jeeps but went into foreign cars after seeing several samples on a trip to New Orleans.

Service is Qvale's secret ingredient. He insists that his agencies provide demonstration rides for prospective customers and offer extensive service facilities, and he spends $30,000 a year to promote auto races to advertise his business. Qvale is so involved in his work that he installed his wife and two sons in a house only four blocks from his office so he does not have to waste time commuting.

Building roomless houses has put James Willis Walter of Tampa in the seven-figure bracket. While working at the age of 23 as a truck driver, Walter read an advertisement for a shell house—that is, four walls and a roof; the buyer builds the rest. Walter and two other men began their own business. Now the company merchandises and finances nearly $10,000,000 in shell houses every year. The Walter family—J.W., his wife and two sons—lives in an eleven-room house with a swimming pool and five television sets (including one in the dining room) a short drive from his office. Walter owns a ranch and belongs to seven clubs, but his young sons each get allowances of only a dollar a week.

An unglamorous aspect of housing brought riches to B. Alden Smith and Compere Loveless, who found their fortunes in sewage disposal. Smith came out of the war a major after a number of missions as a fighter pilot. He met Loveless, a minister's son and engineering graduate, through his father-in-law. In 1946, they pooled their assets of a little cash and a lot of energy and formed Smith & Loveless, Incorporated, a sales organization representing manufacturers in the water and sewage field. Now they run a multi-million-dollar manufacturing operation that turns out prefabricated sewage-disposal equipment.

A flood gave them their first big break. After the disastrous overflow of the Kaw and Missouri Rivers in 1951, the partners were themselves inundated—with debts. They contracted to do all the sewer clean-up in towns along the Kaw, a chore that took a year but was done so well that they established a reputation for dependability. Their first plant, in a Kansas City suburb, was enlarged five times in less than four years. Then they built a second plant. When the Union Tank Car Company acquired the Smith & Loveless facilities, the partners stayed on to run the operations.

Jeno F. Paulucci owes his wealth to his decision to grow bean sprouts without soil. When he was 29, he borrowed $2,500 to start the project. Now he is head of the Chun King Corporation, a $30,000,000 business that processes Oriental foods, wild rice and canned pie fillings.

Paulucci, who believes anyone can triumph over adversity, resigned from a Duluth Junior Achievement group because he thought there was too much emphasis on teamwork and not enough on individuality. The son of an immigrant Italian miner, he had conducted tours through shafts where his father toiled and sold bottles filled with ore as souvenirs. During a recession, he became a grocery commission salesman, living in his automobile and eating sandwiches three times a day. Soon he was selling more groceries than his boss. His next step took him into farming—bean sprouts without soil. He also developed an indoor soil in which to grow mushrooms, which he sold packaged as potting soil. When he wanted wild rice, he airlifted Indians to Manitoban lakelands to harvest it.

A wealthy man at 41, Paulucci considers retirement far away, but he devotes considerable effort to training the young executives around him. He found that the best way to develop talent among these young men was to stay away from the plant for months at a time, leaving them on their own.

There are other classes of millionaires—the "eggheads" and the heirs. Fortune magazine, in a survey, estimated that there were about 100 men who fell in the category of egghead millionaire, the new breed of tycoon who has thought his way to riches. The common denominator of the 100 is a singular lack of interest in their wealth. All were in their 30's or early 40's when they prospered. They were scientists who became industrialists, but originally they had set out to be school teachers or researchers, dreaming of eventually earning around $10,000 a year. The Cold War, the space age and demands for an increase in the nation's brain power set these men on new paths. They were propelled to riches by a common desire for independence and by their self-confidence, but they also were idea men.

As they rose on the economic ladder, most of these egghead tycoons stayed in the modest homes they had bought when they dedicated their lives to research or teaching. Most of them drive rattletrap cars and dress indifferently, if not sloppily.

Heirs to great fortunes have proven that they, too, can succeed though rich. The young men called "scions" in tabloid newspapers used to make names for themselves largely in the gossip columns. Now it is the rare young heir who falls into this category. The Rockefeller brothers—John D. III, Nelson, Winthrop, Laurance and David—Henry Ford II and his brothers and the foremost heirs of them all, the sons of Joseph P. Kennedy, have dedicated their lives to the industrial and social welfare of the country. The Rockefeller family has made a career of giving money away to those who can put it to the best use. Public service is another of their contributions. Nelson is Governor of New York and Winthrop is prominent in Arkansas politics. Their children, as they grow up, are entering the family "business" of putting the fortune of John D. Rockefeller Sr. to work for humanity. John D. IV lived in Buddhist austerity in Tokyo while going to school there to prepare for the United States Foreign Service. Nelson's son, Stephen, entered divinity school, and one of his daughters married a clergyman who was jailed as an integrationist Freedom Rider in the South.

Former Governor Thomas E. Dewey's son, Thomas Jr., a graduate of Princeton and the Harvard Business School, is with a large New York banking house and serves as a director for a school for disturbed boys, a trustee of a hospital and a director of community centers. Robert M. Morgenthau, son of former Secretary of the Treasury Henry Morgenthau Jr., became the third generation of his family to hold public office when President Kennedy named him United States Attorney for the Southern District of New York. G. Mennen Williams, heir to a toilet goods fortune, has devoted his life to public service, as Governor of Michigan and later as a member of President Kennedy's New Frontier.

The sons of Clint W. Murchison Sr. could have relaxed for

the rest of their lives on his Texas oil fortune, but John, at 39, and Clint Jr., at 37, won control of the huge Alleghany Corporation in one of the biggest corporate proxy fights in history. They entered business together by purchasing a publishing house. Clint Jr., with a master's degree from MIT, and John, a graduate of Yale, admittedly "lost our shirts" in uranium and electronics but went on to recoup by winning Alleghany, one of whose holdings was the New York Central Railroad.

What makes the young tycoons tick? Some of the already rich men may want to disprove the old theory that it is three generations from shirtsleeves to shirtsleeves. Perhaps they want to prove that they are smarter than the old man. Just as possibly, they may want to show the old man that the younger generation is—in the jargon of astronauts—"A-O.K." It seems apparent that all the young tycoons, whether self-made or not, are in a hurry to accomplish something in a precarious world.

There is no formula for the progress of these hurrying young men. There are some characteristics that many have in common, however, which could lead one to conclude that all of them might very well have succeeded regardless of their economic beginnings. Many are the sons of immigrants who even today still have "the American dream." Some have leaped from the pages of Horatio Alger. The demands of science have given quite a few their fast starts. The war was a factor, too; men who had faced death were not afraid to take risks in the civilian world. They also wanted to make up for the time they had lost to wartime destruction. Money in itself seldom seems to be the goal of the new tycoon. Rather it is achievement, inventing something new, plowing new ground or becoming powerful and influential. The money obviously is welcome, even by those who are reluctant to live up to it, but status comes more in accomplishment than in owning a million dollars.

.17.

Not the End
– A Beginning

WHEN JOHN F. KENNEDY, YOUNGEST MAN ELECTED TO THE Presidency, wants confidential advice, he is most likely to turn to a Phi Beta Kappa from Nebraska who is eleven years his junior, or possibly his younger brother, who became Attorney General when only 35. They are the "younger statesmen" of the upbeat generation.

Of the key men on the White House staff, ten of the most important were in their 30's when they became New Frontiersmen. Theodore C. Sorensen, who as special counsel may be the man closest to the President, was 32 when he took up his post. Pierre Salinger, the White House press secretary, was 35. Richard N. Goodwin, at 30, became an assistant special counsel to the President.

There were older and perhaps in some ways wiser men on the New Frontier to be sure, including Luther Hodges, who at 63 became Secretary of Commerce, and Dean Rusk, who at 51 was named Kennedy's Secretary of State. However, the average age of the New Frontiersmen was 46 at the start of the Kennedy Administration.

Despite public exclamations over the youth of the official family, it still was not the youngest group to move into the nation's executive suite. George Washington was an old soldier

when he became the first President, but he surrounded himself
with able young men. Thomas Jefferson was in his early thirties
when he wrote the first draft of the Declaration of Independence, a masterpiece. John Adams was just past 40 when he
emerged as a leader of the new nation. James Madison, the
fourth President, was under 30 when he went to the Continental
Congress, and James Monroe was only in his twenties. Washington's first cabinet included only one man over 40; the others
were in their thirties.

The country was new, so it was logical for it to have young
leaders. Today, more than 150 years later, the nation has turned
to youth for leadership—or rather, youth has emerged to lead
the nation. With the election of Kennedy (and it would have
been equally true had Nixon been the victor), the Presidency
literally entered the Twentieth Century. Kennedy, the first son
of the century to become President, succeeded the oldest man
ever to leave the White House. Dwight D. Eisenhower, at 70
an old soldier, welcomed the arrival of youth in the forefront
of the national scene. He gave every indication of finding it a
perfectly natural occurrence. It did not seem an indictment of
the old guard but rather a confirmation that youth was growing
up. It was a tacit admission that by sheer force of numbers youth
was destined to share in the decision making, the policy making
and the running of the country in addition to filling its traditional role as fighter and winner of the country's wars.

The United States Constitution, framed by young men, provides that a man may be elected President when only 35 years
old. There is a likelihood that a man so young will be chosen
in this century. Men in their early thirties have recently been
given key responsibilities in higher education as presidents of
Princeton and Ohio State Universities, among others. The first
Americans to explore the moon and the planets will be young
men on whose shoulders will fall unimaginable responsibilities.

We have seen how young men have become heads of corporations and risen to leadership in new industries geared to the
space age, how youth has been entrusted with sensitive jobs

overseas in the Peace Corps, how college students are growing increasingly serious and how young eggheads have a status they have not held since the days of Jefferson, himself an intellectual with many interests.

"The Unforgotten Generation," some persons call the youth of today. "The Found Generation"—sons of the "Lost Generation"—is another phrase that is applied. Other labels would fit equally well—the "Busy Generation," the "Uphearted Generation," the "Upbeat Generation." To a large extent it has triumphed over war, juvenile delinquency (despite what the headline writers say) and frequent misguidance or nonguidance by parents and educators. It is trying hard to triumph over the demands being placed upon it in an era when a bachelor's degree means about what a high school diploma did at the turn of the century. Young people must work harder and faster to measure up to the standards confronting them in a technological age—and, at the same time, they find they are needed increasingly for community efforts and for the gargantuan tasks confronting a nation trying to establish peace in the world.

Call it what you will, this then is the upbeat, uphearted generation:

> *President Kennedy,* not yet 45, presiding over the affairs of the nation in an old-fashioned rocking chair.
>
> *Alan Shepard* returning from the nation's pioneering space flight protesting that the rocket ride had not lasted long enough.
>
> *Newton N. Minow,* 35-year-old chairman of the Federal Communications Commission, taking on the entire television industry with charges that it has created a vast intellectual "wasteland."
>
> *Van Cliburn,* the pianist, giving $8,000 to the Moscow Baptist Church from his earnings on a Soviet concert tour.
>
> *Pat Boone,* the singer, writing books of advice to teen-agers on their problems.
>
> *New York public school children* making a slum-clearance survey and presenting it to the Mayor.
>
> *A 48-year-old New York City Councilman* finding himself with nine opponents for election—all under 40; average age, 34.

A Vassar girl devoting a summer vacation to grinding a tele-
scope lens.

A 12-year-old Long Island boy earning $180 by leading a group
of adults on a tour of Civil War battlefields.

This is youth in orbit. There is no limit to its activities and
nothing is too small for its attention. The upbeatnik defies
definition. He may be a self-made millionaire who publishes
magazines on hot-rodding or a once-penniless, scarcely educated
adventurer who began by raising his last dime to drill an oil
well. Some tycoons, such as Henry Ford II and the Rockefeller
brothers, inherited success but went on to improve in many
ways upon the achievements and riches of their elders. Playboys
—at least millionaire playboys—went out of style with World
War II. There may have been some idle rich left, but most
of them were Tommy Manville.

Youth owes its present status in large part to the men who
fought in World War II and the Korean War. When they came
home it was not to play, and they were no longer boys. By the
millions they resumed their educations: dormitories and fraternity houses were places to study as far as they were concerned,
as more than one brash teen-ager learned from battle-hardened
former G.I.s. College marriages had another sobering effect on
the nation's campuses. And the atomic bomb took some of the
laughter out of everyone's life.

Men who had completed their educations before they went
to war were in a hurry to catch up on their careers when they
returned. Out of their ranks sprang the new millionaires, more
numerous than ever. Girls who had waited for the boys to come
home were in a hurry, too. Thus the rash of young marriages
and the spiraling birth rate.

The younger generation has had a great deal of help in its
forward surge. Schools, foundations, service clubs, social agencies
and individual members of older generations have given material aid and much encouragement that have made it easier for
youth to be upbeat. Prosperity has helped, too.

When a college man was told in the depression days of the 1930's that he would be lucky on graduation if he got a job digging ditches, he did not anticipate it joyfully as a way to contribute to mankind. Today's Peace Corps volunteer, a son of prosperity, regards as a challenge and perhaps even as "fun" the prospect of manual labor in a disease-ridden land at substandard wages as a deterrent to Communism. He can afford this interlude in the knowledge that he will be able to return home and get a job at many times what his ditch-digging father received. The security offered by a child-centered culture may well be the secret ingredient that has produced the self-confident upbeat generation.

Appendix

Some who read this book may wish to obtain more information on specific subjects. With this in view there follows a list of organizations where more details than could be included in a book are available:

Advancement and Placement Institute, specializing in summer jobs, Box 99, Greenpoint Station, Brooklyn 22, New York.

American Jewish Committee, Institute of Human Relations, 165 East 56th Street, New York 22.

American Legion, Post Office Box 1055, Indianapolis 6, Indiana.

American Medical Association, Department of Health Education, 535 North Dearborn Street, Chicago 10.

B'nai B'rith Youth Organization, 1640 Rhode Island Avenue, N.W., Washington 6, D.C.

Boys' Clubs of America, 771 First Avenue, New York 17.

Boy Scouts of America, New Brunswick, New Jersey.

Camp Fire Girls, 65 Worth Street, New York 13.

Census Bureau, Department of Commerce, Washington 25, D.C.

Chamber of Commerce of the United States, 1615 H Street, N.W., Washington 6, D.C.

Civil Service Commission, Washington 25, D.C.

Commission on Youth Service Projects, Room 753, 475 Riverside Drive, New York 27.

Daughters of the American Revolution, 3627 Chesapeake Street, N.W., Washington 8, D.C.

De Molay, International Supreme Council, Southeast Corner, Armour and Warwick Boulevard, Kansas City 11, Missouri.

Eagles, Fraternal Order of, 2401 Wisconsin Avenue, Milwaukee 3, Wisconsin.

Elks Grand Lodge, Order of, 2750 Lake View Avenue, Chicago 14.

Four-H Clubs, Department of Agriculture, Federal Extension Service, Washington 25, D.C.

Four-H Service Committee, Inc., National, 59 East Van Buren Street, Chicago 5.

Fraternities:

National Panhellenic Conference, Mrs. William Nash, 410 Fairfax, Little Rock, Arkansas.

Banta's Greek Exchange, Menasha, Wisconsin.

Dean Fred H. Turner, Interfraternity Research and Advisory Council, 152 Administration Building, Urbana, Illinois.

Fraternity Month, St. Paul 14, Minnesota.

National Interfraternity Council, 15 East 40th Street, New York.

Future Farmers of America, Office of Education, Department of Health, Education and Welfare, Washington 25, D.C.

Future Homemakers of America, Office of Education, Department of Health, Education and Welfare, Washington 25, D.C.

Future Nurses Club, American Nurses Association, 10 Columbus Circle, New York 19.

Girls' Clubs of America, Inc., 22 East 38th Street, New York 17.

Girl Scouts of America, 830 Third Avenue, New York 22.

Jaycees, Junior Chamber of Commerce of the United States, Boulder Park, Box 7, Tulsa 2, Oklahoma.

Jewish Women, National Council of, 1 West 47th Street, New York 36.

Junior Achievement, Inc., 500 Fifth Avenue, New York 36.

Kiwanis International, 101 East Erie Street, Chicago.

Lions International, 209 North Michigan Avenue, Chicago 1.

Luther League of America, 2900 Queen Lane, Philadelphia 29.

Methodist Church, Board of Education, Post Office Box 871, Nashville 2, Tennessee.

Moose, Loyal Order of, Moosehart, Illinois.

National Clean Up, Paint Up, Fix Up Bureau, 1500 Rhode Island Avenue, N.W., Washington 5, D.C.

National Education Association, 1201 16th Street, N.W., Washington 6, D.C.

National Federation of Settlements and Neighborhood Centers, 226 West 47th Street, New York 36.

National Jewish Welfare Board, 145 East 32nd Street, New York 16.

Nutrition:

National Live Stock and Meat Board, 407 South Dearborn Street, Chicago 5.

National Tuberculosis Association, 1790 Broadway, New York 19.

Nutrition Foundation, 99 Park Avenue, New York 16.

American Home Economics Association, 1600 20th Street, N.W., Washington 9, D.C.

American Dietetic Association, 620 North Michigan Avenue, Chicago 11.

National Dairy Council, 11 North Canal Street, Chicago 6.

National Vitamin Foundation, Inc., 149 East 78th Street, New York 21.

National Food Conference, Merchandise Mart, Chicago 54.

Institute of Home Economics, Department of Agriculture Research Service, Washington 25, D.C.

Nutrition Section, Division of Health Services, Social Security Administration, Department of Health, Education and Welfare, Washington 25, D.C.

Optimist International, Railway Exchange Building, St. Louis 1.
Peace Corps, 806 Connecticut Avenue, N.W., Washington 25, D.C.

Purdue University Opinion Poll for Teen-Agers, Lafayette, Indiana.

Recreation Association of America, 8 West Eighth Street, New York 11.

Red Cross, American, Washington 6, D.C.

Rotary International, 1600 Ridge Avenue, Evanston, Illinois.

Soroptimist Federation of the Americas, 1616 Walnut Street, Philadelphia 3.

Student Association, National, 3457 Chestnut Street, Philadelphia 4.

UNICEF, United States Committee for, United Nations, New York.

United Church of Christ, 287 Park Avenue South, New York 10.

YMCA, National Council of, 291 Broadway, New York.

Young Presidents Organization, Inc., 375 Park Avenue, New York 22.

YWCA, National, 600 Lexington Avenue, New York 22.

Bibliography

Advancement and Placement Institute, *Summer Jobs,* a listing of more than 14,000 national and international posts, 1961.

American College Health Association, *Proceedings of the Fourth National Conference on Health in Colleges,* 1954.

Banta's Greek Exchange, an interfraternity journal, January, 1961, issue.

Baskin, Samuel, *Quest for Quality, New Dimensions in Higher Education, No. 7,* Department of Health, Education and Welfare.

Batten, Charles E. and McLean, Donald E., *Fit to Be Tied,* Seabury Press.

B'nai B'rith Youth Organization, *A Manual for Young Adult Members,* "Girls Member's Manual" and "Inside Information for Members of Aleph Zadik Aleph."

Boone, Pat, *'Twixt Twelve and Twenty,* Prentice-Hall, Inc.

Boone, Pat, *Between You, Me and the Gatepost,* Prentice-Hall, Inc.

Boys' Clubs of America, Needs and Interests of Adolescent Boys' Club Members, report on the national survey of members aged 14 to 18, 1960.

Boy Scouts of America, *Merit Badge Series on Radio, Cooking, Automobiling, Aviation, Electricity, Camping and Citizenship.* Boy Scout Requirements, 1961.

Buckler, Helen; Fiedler, Mary F., and Allen, Martha F., *Wo-He-Lo, the Story of Camp Fire Girls,* Holt, Rinehart and Winston.

Camp Fire Girls, Inc., *The Book of the Camp Fire Girls.*

Census Bureau of the United States, 1960 Census reports on farm population, population characteristics, general population characteristics, school enrollment, literacy and educational attainment, household and family characteristics, marital status and family status.

Cole, William Graham, *Sex and Love in the Bible,* Association Press.

Coleman, Elnora H. and Green, Reginald H., *Student Responsibility in Advising, Counselling and Tutoring; Entering the Academic Vocation—What Can Students Do?; Student Contributions to Institutional Self-Study,* National Student Association.

Coleman, James S., *Social Climates in High Schools,* Department of Health, Education and Welfare.

Commission on Youth Service Projects, "Invest Your Summer," *Catalog of Service Opportunities,* 1961.

Cornell, Betty, *All About Boys; Glamour Guide for Teens; Teen-Age Popularity Guide,* Prentice-Hall, Inc.

D'Evelyn, Katherine, *Meeting Children's Emotional Needs, A Guide for Teachers,* Prentice-Hall, Inc.

De Marche, Edythe and David, *Handbook of Co-ed Teen Activities,* Association Press.

Duvall, Evelyn M., *Facts of Life and Love for Teen-Agers,* Association Press; *Keeping Up with Teen-Agers,* "Public Affairs Pamphlet No. 127," Public Affairs Committee, Inc.

Duvall, Evelyn M. and Sylvanus M., *Sex Ways—in Fact and Faith: Bases for Christian Family Policy,* Association Press.

Ellzey, W. Clark, *Sex, Love, and Marriage,* Department of Family Life, National Council of the Churches of Christ in the U.S.A.

Fairchild, Roy W. and Wynn, John Charles, *Families in the Church: a Protestant Survey,* Association Press.

Four-H Foods and Nutrition Development Committee, *Improving Teen-Age Nutrition,* Department of Agriculture.

Freedman, Mervin B., "Some Observations on Personality Development in College Women," *Student Medicine,* February, 1960, Volume 8, Number 3; *Impact of College, New Dimensions in Higher Education No. 4,* Department of Health, Education and Welfare.

Gebhard, Paul H.; Pomeroy, Wardell B.; Martin, Clyde E., and Christenson, Cornelia V., *Pregnancy, Birth and Abortion,* Harper & Brothers and Paul B. Hoeber, Inc.

Gilbert, Eugene, *Advertising and Marketing to Young People,* Printers' Ink Books.

Gillespie, James M., and Allport, Gordon W., *Youth's Outlook on the Future,* Doubleday & Company, Inc.

Girl Scouts of the U.S.A., "Girl Scout Handbook" and "Senior Girl Scouting."

Gleazer, Edmund J. Jr., "An Introduction to Junior Colleges," American Association of Junior Colleges.

Goodman, Paul, "Youth in the Organized Society, Growing Up in America," *Commentary,* February, 1960.

Green, Reginald H., *Better Education for More College Students, Backgrounds and Bases for Student Responsibility,* National Student Association.

Gregg, Walter H., *A Boy and His Physique,* National Dairy Council.

Hillman, Arthur, *Neighborhood Centers Today,* National Federation of Settlements and Neighborhood Centers.

Hulme, William E., *Face Your Life With Confidence,* Counsels for Youth; *God, Sex & Youth,* Christian Counsels for Young People on Their Problems of Sex, Prentice-Hall, Inc.

Hymes, James L. Jr., "How to Tell Your Child About Sex," *Public Affairs Pamphlet No. 149,* Public Affairs Committee. *Effective Home-School Relations,* Prentice-Hall, Inc.

Jackson, Joyce, *Guide to Dating,* Prentice-Hall, Inc.

Johnson, Willard, and Coleman, Eleanor, *Student Responsibility in Higher Education,* National Student Association.

Kelly, The Very Rev. Monsignor George A., *The Catholic Youth's Guide to Life and Love,* Random House.

Knight, Douglas M., et al, *The Federal Government and Higher Education,* Prentice-Hall, Inc.

Landers, Ann, *Since You Ask Me,* Prentice-Hall, Inc.

Landis, Judson T. and Mary G., *Teen-Agers Guide for Living,* Prentice-Hall, Inc.; *Youth and Marriage,* a Student Manual, Prentice-Hall, Inc.

Landis, Paul H., "Teenage Adjustments in Large and Small Families," *Bulletin 549, April, 1954,* Washington State College; "Coming of Age: Problems of Teen-Agers," *Public Affairs Pamphlet No. 234,* Public Affairs Committee, Inc.

Lee, Alfred McClung, *Fraternities Without Brotherhood,* Beacon Press.

Lerrigo, Marion O., and Southard, Helen, a series of sex education pamphlets entitled "Story About You," "Facts Aren't Enough," "Finding Yourself," "Parents' Privilege" and "Preparation for

Marriage"; American Medical Association and distributed with the National Education Association.

Leverton, Ruth M., *A Girl and Her Figure,* National Dairy Council.

Loeb, Robert H. Jr., *She-Manners; He-Manners,* Association Press.

Michigan, University of, *A Study of Adolescent Boys,* 1955, for the National Council, Boy Scouts of America; *A Study of Boys Becoming Adolescents,* 1960, for the National Council, Boy Scouts of America; *Adolescent Girls,* 1958, for the Girl Scouts of the U.S.A.

Morse, Arthur D., *Schools of Tomorrow—Today,* Doubleday.

National Association of Student Councils, *The Student Council in the Secondary School,* National Association of Secondary-School Principals.

National Education Association, *NEA Handbook,* 1960-61.

National Interfraternity Conference: *Fiftieth Anniversary Yearbook,* 1959; *1960 Yearbook; Interfraternity Views and News,* September, 1961; *Minutes of the National Interfraternity Conference of 1960.*

Osborne, Ernest G., *The Teen-Agers' Pocket Guide to Understanding Your Parents,* Association Press.

Public Affairs Press, *The New Frontiersmen—Profiles of the Men Around Kennedy.*

Purdue University, Division of Educational Reference, Reports of Poll No. 53 on *Future Parents' Views on Child Management;* Poll No. 55 on *Teenagers' Attitudes Toward Teenage Culture,* and Poll No. 62 on *Youth's Attitudes Toward Courtship and Marriage.*

Reinhold, Meyer, *Barron's Teen-Age Summer Guide,* Barron's Educational Series, Inc.

Rice, Thurman B., M.D., a series of sex education pamphlets first issued by the American Medical Association in 1933, entitled "In Training," for boys of high school age; "Those First Sex Questions," "How Life Goes On and On" and "The Age of Romance."

Riesman, David; Jacob, Philip E., and Sanford, Nevitt, *Spotlight on the College Student,* American Council on Education.

Roberts, Dorothy M., *Partners With Youth,* Association Press.

Scott, C. Winfield; Hill, Clyde M., and Burns, Hobert W., *The Great Debate, Our Schools in Crisis,* Prentice-Hall, Inc.

Simon, Marion, editor, *A World in Transition, Students in Action,* 1960-61 Codification of Policy of the National Student Association.

Stanford, Edward V., O.S.A., *Preparing for Marriage,* Mentzer, Bush.

Suydam, Margaret, ". . . And She Does It So Easily and So Well," National Dairy Council.

Thomas, John L., S.J., "The Catholic Family," The America Press, reprinted from *Social Order,* and *The American Catholic Family,* Prentice-Hall, Inc.

Trecker, Audrey R. and Harleigh B., *Handbook of Community Service Projects,* Association Press.

Wall Street Journal, *The New Millionaires and How They Made Their Fortunes,* Bernard Geis Associates.

White House Conference on Children and Youth, "Reference Papers on Children and Youth, 1960"; "Survey Papers on Children and Youth in the 1960's"; "The States Report on Children and Youth in the 1960's"; "Focus on Children and Youth, Report of National Organizations, 1960."

Wise, W. Max, *They Come for the Best of Reasons—College Students Today,* American Council on Education.

World Council of Churches, *Summer Service Bulletin, 1961.*

Wynn, John Charles, *How Christian Parents Face Family Problems,* Westminster Press.

Index

Index